THE MYTHS
THAT MAKE US

THE MYTHS
THAT MAKE US

JULIE HUNTER

HAZARD PRESS
publishers

Published by Hazard Press Limited
P.O. Box 2151, Christchurch, New Zealand
Email: info@hazard.co.nz
www.hazardpress.co.nz

Copyright © Julie Hunter 2006
First published 2006

The author has asserted her moral rights in the work.

This book is copyright. Except for the purposes of fair reviewing, no part of this publication (whether it be in any eBook, digital, electronic or traditionally printed format or otherwise) may be reproduced or transmitted in any form or by any means, electronic, digital or mechanical, including CD, DVD, eBook, PDF format, photocopying, recording, or any information storage and retrieval system, including by any means via the internet or World Wide Web, or by any means yet undiscovered, without permission in writing from the publisher. Infringers of copyright render themselves liable to prosecution.

ISBN 1-877393-13-4

Cover illustration *Adam Accusing Eve*, 16th–17th-century Flemish tapestry. Galleria d'Arte Antica e Moderna, Florence. Photograph: Alinari

Cover design by Graeme Hobbs

Printed in New Zealand

CONTENTS

Author's note	6
Acknowledgements	7
List of Illustrations	8
Introduction	11
1. Myths	13
2. Sumer	23
3. Babylonia	41
4. Abraham and his Descendants	49
5. Jesus	71
6. Christianity	85
7. Mystics	99
Appendix One: The Gospel of Thomas	112
Appendix Two: The Nicene Creed	122
Appendix Three: Meditation	123
Endnotes	125
Bibliography	129
Index	133

AUTHOR'S NOTE

The biblical translation used is the Revised Standard Version, unless otherwise stated.

Where the words 'man' or 'men' have been used in quotations, they are taken to mean 'humanity'.

BCE (before the common era) and CE (common era) are used instead of the interchangeable BC and AD.

ACKNOWLEDGEMENTS

To Peter Cammock for the inspiration.

To Michael Harlow, who took my awful first draft and guided me through three more drafts, to the stage that the manuscript could be presented to publishers.

To Marc Jarman who encouraged me all the way.

To the Student Assistants at the Oriental Institute Museum, University of Chicago, for finding many images for me.

To Anne Baring and the Westar Institute, for permission to use images from their books *The Myth of the Goddess* and *The Five Gospels*.

To Wim van den Dungen and many museums, galleries, and photographic studios who reduced their fees for me.

To the many people who read the manuscript and took the time to write comments – some complimentary and some not. All their comments were useful, and many of the suggested improvements have been incorporated.

To Bob Stoothoff, who polished the text well beyond his brief.

To Hazard Press, who gave me the opportunity to publish. I learnt what a long, intensive process this is.

To Katy Sinton, who copy-edited the text to as near perfection as possible.

To my daemon who had me at the right place at the right time, and guided me to some very special people.

LIST OF ILLUSTRATIONS

Fig. 1:   Table of civilisations, drawn by Mark Pickering.   10

Fig. 2:   Map of the area from Greece to Persia, drawn by Mark Pickering.   25

Fig. 3:   Ziggurat, drawn by Marc Jarman.   26

Fig. 4a: *Warka Vase*. National Museum of Iraq, Baghdad. Photograph: Hirmer Verlag.   26

Fig. 4b: *The Sacred Marriage*, courtesy of the Oriental Institute of the University of Chicago.   27

Fig. 5:   Yin and Yang, drawn by Mark Pickering.   28

Fig. 6:   *Enki*, drawn by Robin Baring after cylinder seal impression in J. Hawkes, *The First Great Civilisations: Life in Mesopotamia, the Indus Valley and Egypt*, p. 36. Permission granted by Anne Baring.   29

Fig. 7:   *Warka Head*, National Museum of Iraq, Baghdad. Photograph: Hirmer Verlag.   31

Fig. 8:   *Asclepius and Hygieia*, National Museums Liverpool, World Museum Liverpool.   32

Fig. 9:   *The Tree of Life*, copyright the Trustees of the British Museum.   33

Fig. 10: *Stele of Hammurabi*, Musée du Louvre, Paris. Photograph: RMN/Hervé Lewandowski.   39

Fig. 11: *Marduk slaying Tiamat*, copyright the Trustees of the British Museum.   43

Fig. 12: Babylonian Empire, drawn by Mark Pickering.p47   47

Fig. 13: Gold pendant, Musée du Louvre, Paris. Photograph: RMN/Droits réservés.   53

Fig. 14: Statuette of a snake goddess, early Aegean, Minoan, Bronze Age, Late Minoan I Period, about 1600–1500 BCE or early 20th century BCE. Object place: Greece; thought to be from Crete. Gold, ivory. Height 16.1 cm (6 5/16 in). Museum of Fine Arts, Boston. Gift of Mrs W. Scott Fitz, 14.863.   56

Fig. 15: Slinger, copyright the Trustees of the British Museum.   57

Fig. 16: Israel and Judah, drawn by Mark Pickering.   59

Fig. 17a: Alabaster panel left, copyright the Trustees of the British Museum.   60

Fig. 17b: Alabaster panel right, copyright the Trustees of the British Museum.   61

Fig. 18: Persian Empire, drawn by Mark Pickering.   62

Fig. 19: Persian cylinder seal, copyright the Trustees of the British Museum.   63

Fig. 20: Palestine. From Robert W. Funk, Roy W. Hoover, and the Jesus Seminar, *The Five Gospels*, p. xxii. Permission granted by the Westar Institute.   75

Fig. 21: Writing timetable, drawn by Mark Pickering.   79

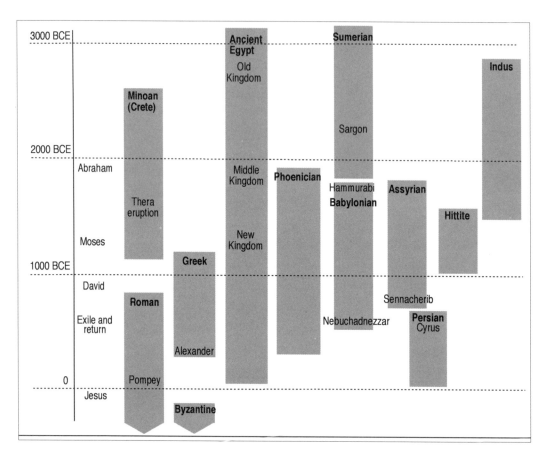

Figure 1: Table of civilisations.

INTRODUCTION

It is a myth, not a mandate ... by which men are moved.
— Irwin Edman

At a family Christmas dinner I heard a man say, 'It's a pity there were not more goddesses in mythology.' I was aghast. Had he not heard of the great Greek goddesses? Had he not read the writings of Joseph Campbell, the mythologist? Strangely, this man gave lectures on leadership based on the work of Campbell. No wonder some of his female students accused him of male chauvinism. I rushed home from the dinner determined to write an article for him about the power and status of ancient goddesses.

I soon became fascinated with my research. I discovered that Greece was not the cradle of European civilisation, as I had believed: that cradle was Sumer, now southern Iraq. Its flowering predates both Greece's splendour and the writing of the Old Testament by up to 2000 years. Sumer's influence spread east and west from approximately 3000 BCE until it was incorporated into Babylonia about 2000 BCE. Babylonia's capital city, Babylon, was the greatest city in the ancient world. During its flourishing 2500 year period, Sumer/Babylonia influenced all the surrounding nations – from India to Crete, and from there on to Greece – with its weaving, metalwork and masonry industries, its vast trading, written script, codes of law, myths and religion. *See Fig. 1, p.10*

Some of Sumer's myths found their way into the biblical books of Genesis and Exodus. This is not surprising since Abraham left Ur of the Chaldeans (Babylonians) about 2000 BCE, taking with him myths that were later adapted to fit the needs of the Hebrews. So Sumer was not only the cradle of Western civilisation, but also the cradle of its religions.

I had struggled with Christianity most of my life, finding the Old Testament too violent with its emphasis on sin and punishment, and the New Testament unbelievable. Yet I knew there was something deeply religious in me, so I started investigating other Near Eastern myths, particularly creation myths. What I found in the ancient beliefs of Sumer was a completely different way of looking at life. Instead of sin and punishment, Sumerian myths emphasise the unity of all beings, and so the culture was tolerant and peaceful. They also feature strong creation goddesses, reflected in the fact that women in Sumer had equality.

In the 20th century it became possible to study the history of the Near East alongside the myths of that area. The research I ventured into has broadened my understanding, and reinforced beliefs I was barely aware of within myself, giving them a firm foundation. I was constantly surprised with what I found, particularly how closely ancient myths blend with many streams of modern psychological thought.

My journey progressed from ignorance, through fascination, to understanding. I hope I can pass on some of that understanding, and some of the wonder of my discoveries.

The individual merely offers his contribution, and in this sense only do I dare to speak of my way of seeing things.
– Carl G. Jung

MYTHS

Myths are public dreams, dreams are private myths.
– Joseph Campbell

PERSONAL MYTHS

In 1993 I founded a company that was contracted by the Accident Compensation Corporation, New Zealand's national accident insurance organisation, to get their clients back to work. Unable to return to their previous jobs because of their injuries and pain, they had been unemployed and unemployable for up to 12 years, some on compensation payments of over $1,000 a week. A basic belief of mine was that many people are forced into jobs they hate whilst knowing, deep down, what kind of work could bring them happiness. Following this belief, we concentrated on what these people really wanted to do, what they dreamed of doing. There was a top executive who wanted to run a dairy with his wife, a secretary who wanted to work with children, a computer operator who wanted to be a tour guide, a butcher who wanted to work with computers, a roofer who wanted to cook, a factory worker who wanted to drive a taxi, a labourer who wanted a high-paying, dirty, hard job in the railways with his brother ... the list goes on and on. We made these jobs happen for them, helping each to fulfil their dream, and their pain became manageable, sometimes miraculously disappearing. It was magic to watch – they totally changed from downcast and pained to uplifted and joyful. Not only did they become happy, hard-working employees, but their families found them pleasant to live with. Their dreams, the inner knowledge of themselves and who they wanted to be – their *personal myths* – were on the way to being fulfilled.

The feedback we consistently received from these people was that we listened to them, and in many cases we were the first people who had ever listened to them. They had repeatedly been told what was appropriate for them to do by family, teachers, friends and society. They were not listening to their inner wisdom, and had been discouraged from following their personal myths, so that they had struggled and failed to become the person other people expected them to be. They had been on the wrong track, doing the wrong thing, not fulfilling their dreams, and so were not able to realise their potential. It was no wonder their bodies would not heal. For if they had healed, they would have had to return to a lifestyle they hated – a lifestyle that was contrary to what they knew, deep down, was where their potential, calling and happiness lay. They were demonstrating the powerful unconscious link between mind and body, the link between their inner selves and the outer lives they had been living. We stepped in as 'fairy godmothers' and helped them re-find their own personal myths – strange as those myths may have seemed to anyone else. Sometimes the myth was buried so deep we had to 'dig' it out of them, as they had learned that talking about it often led to ridicule – 'You're not bright enough to do that!', 'You'll never make an adequate living out of that!' They had become ashamed of what they were and what they wanted to do with their lives. We encouraged them to trust the wisdom of their inner selves, to reconnect their mind and body and so become whole, healed and healthy. Their joy and reason for living had returned to them – their lives gained meaning and purpose.

When I sold the company and started my research, I found that the idea of a personal myth, an inner dream, was over 2000 years old. In the 4th century BCE the great Greek philosopher Plato wrote that our souls, which are immortal, choose a unique life pattern and purpose, and then pass through a forgetting process before we are born. A guardian spirit, a 'daemon', is the soul's companion, and this spirit remembers our purpose and guides us towards it.[1] (The notion of *daemon* is clearly connected with the Christian idea of *guardian angel*.) Plato recommended living in accordance with this myth for a happy, healthy life. It explains in story form the difference between those who find fulfilment in life and those who do not. Using symbols similar to those found in dreams – in Plato's case a daemon acting as a guide – myths provide a model for human belief and behaviour. They explain the mysteries of life in terms we can understand.

In the 20th century the myth Plato told surfaced again, this time in the new field of psychology. Carl Jung, the founder of analytic psychology, placed the daemon with the soul at the centre of our unconscious, accessible to all who wish to seek and find them.* He said we all have our own personal myth: 'It is what is commonly called

---

* Jung's work has been influential in psychiatry, psychology, the study of religion, mythology, literature, and related fields. For example, many personality/psychological tests, particularly the Myers Briggs, are based on Jung's theories, and workers in the relatively new field of Consciousness Research frequently quote Jung's work.

vocation: ... Anyone with a vocation hears the voice of the inner man: he is *called*. That is why the legends say that he possesses a private daemon who counsels him and whose mandates he must obey.'[2] Jung suggested that the psychological 'ills' of humankind are the result of our ignoring the daemon of our personal myth. Suppression of the daemon unleashes activities within the unconscious such as unpleasant dreams, and may lead to depression, verbal and physical violence, accident-proneness, pain and illness. The denied daemon becomes a demon. Those who do not heed the inner voice are susceptible to the outer voices of family, friends and society, and may be influenced by the strong voices of unscrupulous leaders. Jung recommended, like Plato, hearing and following one's inner daemon for a fulfilled life. He brought the personal myth of each individual into modern-day psychology.

The pagan myth Plato recommended in the 4th century BCE has been adopted by many in the healing professions today, for example, the American surgeon and writer Bernie Siegel, who writes:

> I believe that within that fertilized egg is an inner message, an inner awareness that says, 'This is your path, this is how you can be the best human being possible.' If you follow it, you will achieve your full growth and full potential as a human being before you let go of the Tree of Life ... whether you die at two or a hundred and two. If you don't you will become psychologically or spiritually troubled. And if that doesn't call your attention back to your path, your body will become physically ill.[3]

Such is the personal myth, the wisdom within that knows the path which will bring fulfilment. Jung found most of his patients were seeking that path. In mythological terms they had completed their hero/heroine journey – that is, they had moved emotionally away from parents to form their own relationships and establish themselves in the world. Although they had attained what society dictated would make them happy in life, be it wealth, power, success, recognition or whatever, they realised there was something missing – what they had acquired did not fulfil them. They had spent all the time exercising their rational, thinking intellect, and neglected their innate, intuitive wisdom. Most of Jung's patients were aged over 35, intelligent and considered successful in worldly terms. They were seeking the meaning of their existence, the purpose of their lives. Jung believed they were seeking 'wholeness' – the healing of conflict within themselves that would bring serenity and harmony. They achieved this by taking notice of the unconscious, the inner world that presents itself in dreams and the imagination, and by respecting its dictates. Jung believed this is a spiritual quest or journey: a quest to find the meaning and purpose of life. Having supreme value, it can only be described as 'religious'. Jung recognised the linguistic connection between the words 'whole', 'heal', 'health' and '*holy*': they all come from the Germanic word *hailaz*, which means whole. By allowing the powerful unconscious into consciousness, inner conflicts are healed and we become psychologically healthy and whole, forming a 'holiness' similar to that found in children. Jung wrote: 'Originally we were born out of a world of wholeness and in the first years of life are still completely contained in it. There we have knowledge without knowing it.'[4] The wise man Jesus recognised this when he said of children 'to such belongs the kingdom of God' (Mark: 10:14, Matthew 19:14, Luke: 18:16). (In the Hebrew world the word 'God' was too holy to speak, and so the gospel of Matthew, the most Jewish gospel, uses the word 'Heaven' in place of the word 'God'.)

At a time when religion in the West no longer meets the needs of many people, it may seem strange to find the word 'holiness' in the secular field of psychology. But holiness or wholeness is central to Jung's psychology. Although our society is increasingly irreligious we still seek a wise force to guide us, and that force is to be found not outside ourselves, as in many religions, but inside us, as in ancient philosophy and mysticism. The Greeks had a word for it: *enthousiasmos*, the divinity within.* We do not have such a word in the English language, suggesting that it is not part of our cultural heritage.

Plato reasoned that the soul is immortal and eternal, and long ago learned all truth. It needs only to be reminded of these truths for knowledge to emerge – knowledge is 'recollection' from the soul. In 1939 Jung wrote:

> As a matter of fact we have actually known everything all along; for all these things are always there, only we are not there for them. The possibility of the deepest insight [sight from within] existed at all times, but we were always too far away from it.[5]

---

* The English word enthusiasm comes from the Greek word *enthousiasmos*: it originally meant 'inspired', 'possessed by a god'.

He called this inherited insight, knowledge or wisdom the *collective unconscious*: the 'part of the psyche which retains and transmits the common psychological inheritance of mankind'.[6] With memories going back thousands of years the collective unconscious produces myths, images, dreams and religious ideas that are common throughout Western Christian culture. These communications from deep within use primordial images that are still alive with meaning today, which Jung called *archetypes*. From his extensive study of myths, legends and fairy tales he found that archetypes recurring in these stories were the same as those appearing in his patients' and his own dreams. He wrote that dreams contain 'numberless interconnections to which one can find parallels only in mythological associations of ideas'.[7] An archetype found in myth is the same and means the same as that archetype in an exceptional dream or religious icon. For example, Plato's daemon and today's guardian angel are the same in myth, artwork, dream and religion – they are guides.

COLLECTIVE MYTHS

Because of this psychological/spiritual connection, myths carry within them tremendous power. The most powerful myth of all is a creation myth. It is the ultimate symbolic story a culture has about itself, a *collective myth*, describing the sacred and spiritual origin of the culture and bonding the people together in a common beginning. Religions are founded on creation myths, rituals are centred in them, societies live by them, the ethics of right and wrong are embedded within them, and laws are created from them. Not only are they collective, for all the people of a culture, they also form the foundation for personal myths – the hopes, dreams and aspirations of individuals within that culture. But creation myths tell what is acceptable and unacceptable behaviour only at a particular time and place. The culture of contemporary Western society is based on the creation myth in Genesis 2–4. This myth has not changed in 3,000 years, and yet we are a long way from tribal semi-nomads following pasture for our animals in a land beset by large tracts of desert. These wandering tribal people were united by a single, all-powerful male creator, Yahweh. He demanded obedience and would benefit those following his demands and punish those who did not. The mythologised history of the Hebrews connects Yahweh with his 'chosen' people through his prophet Moses. Yahweh promised the Hebrews the land of Canaan and the destruction of those deemed enemies as long as they remained faithful to him and him alone. He became their tribal war God, stamping out all who stood in their path. In this way the disparate Hebrew tribes were bonded together into a single, cohesive, conquering nation.

The message of Jesus was different. Finding the kingdom of God was the central and dominant theme of his teaching: 'The kingdom of God is in the midst of you' (Luke 17:21). (Note that the King James and New International translations have 'The kingdom of God is within you'.) He taught the concept of divinity within and, following from that, love for all humanity: 'Love your enemies' (Matthew 5:44). In other words, he taught not only the Greek idea of *enthousiasmos*, but also their idea of *agape* – love for all humanity, including enemies. But the teachings of Jesus were taken to the West by Paul, who was steeped in the old Judaic traditions of his time. Paul, a Pharisee, never met Jesus or heard him speak, and had little contact with Jesus' inner circle of disciples in Jerusalem. So we have Pauline Christianity in the West based on the creation myth of a distant Father Creator God, banishment from the presence of this God because of the sin of Adam, and the need for the sacrifice of Jesus to re-establish the bond with the Father. Jesus taught none of this.

Through the power of the Genesis creation myth we have inherited an omnipotent male creator as central to Christianity. There is no hint of the female element symbolising nurture and compassion. According to Marie-Louise von Franz, an authority on the psychological interpretation of fairy tales, the feminine in any story represents feelings, emotions, instincts, the irrational, the 'loving' way people relate to one another. If the male principle is not balanced by the female then access to these unconscious attributes is blocked.[8]

Not only is the Genesis creator exclusively male, he is removed and separate from his creatures – the divinity is transcendent, far away, untouchable and unknowable by humanity. Sin was introduced and the supreme sin of Adam was disobedience ('Thou shalt not') with 'righteous' punishment for disobedience meted out by the authoritarian father. This is the creation myth much of Western civilisation and its values is built on. It has been carried into laws, customs, practices and even into family households.

By human historical standards the Genesis myth is relatively new, about 3,000 years old. There were earlier creation myths from the same area, from cultures far older and more advanced than that of the Hebrews. These older myths existed before and alongside the Genesis myth in the ancient Near East. They had an equal female element, taking humanity to be moulded from and/or born of a female deity. Humans were created to assist the deities in their work on earth and there was no hint of sin. Such creation myths produced societies very different from those founded on the Hebrew creation myth. Not only were the older religions and rituals different but so were their values and laws. Among the most significant differences were religious and ethnic tolerance, married women possessing their own property (which did not start to happen in the West until the 19th century CE), and women taking an active part in religion and rituals (which was not permitted in the West until the 20th century CE, and then only in some churches).

Such differences of belief separated the small number of Hebrews from the established sophisticated civilisations around them. Nevertheless the ancient Hebrews adapted the myths and stories of these civilisations, particularly those of Sumer, for their own mythologised history. Abraham, the 'father' of Judaism, Christianity and Islam came from Sumer, known as Shinar in the Bible. Today Sumer is recognised in historical terms as the cradle of Western civilisation. What is less well known is that Sumer is also the cradle of its religions. Abraham took the myths and stories of Sumer with him when he travelled from the city of Ur to Canaan. Exploring Sumer's myths along with its history leads into our religious heritage. Creation myths form the power base of a culture and when the culture needs a change of attitude the creation myth changes to suit what is required.

Not until the 20th century has the ancient history of the Near East become well known in the West. Increased interest in archaeology, anthropology, sociology, psychology, mythology and philosophy, how they mesh together and how they affect religions and cultures, has sharpened awareness that there might be other, older, wiser beliefs that could help us in our global world today. The older creation myths, particularly of Sumer and Babylonia, produced tolerant, inclusive cultures, whereas the Genesis myth produced a culture with divisions between races, nations, religions, gender, families and even within families. Going back as far as we can to the first written creation myth we have, the Sumerian *Eridu Genesis*, we can see what was important to these ancient peoples.

SUMER

IN THE BEGINNING... THE WORLD MOUNTAIN

In the 4th millennium BCE, over 1000 years before Abraham and 2000 years before Moses, Sumer had a rich civilisation and culture. Today Sumer is recognised as the first of the great civilisations, the cradle of European culture. Situated in the area known as the Fertile Crescent between the Tigris and Euphrates rivers, Sumer was in biblical Garden of Eden territory. 'A river flowed out of Eden to water the garden, and there it divided and became four rivers... The name of the third river is Tigris ... The fourth river is the Euphrates' (Genesis 2:10ff.). These two great rivers made the land fertile and the Sumerians widened and controlled its natural fertility with intricately engineered irrigation canals and channels. It is no wonder it was the biblical place of 'Paradise' with its green and pleasant land, flourishing economy, sophisticated arts and crafts, and settled, peaceful society.

See Fig. 2, p. 25

All high civilisations have a system of writing and the Sumerians had the earliest known form of written script – cuneiform – in which objects were represented by simplified pictures. Cuneiform script spread from Sumer throughout the Near and Middle East. Surviving clay tablets provide us with much of the knowledge we have of these ancient times. The earliest known creation myth, *Eridu Genesis*, was found on one such Sumerian clay tablet. As creation myths are the foundation of a culture, expressing the values and beliefs within that culture, *Eridu Genesis* tells us much about the Sumerians. Their society was based on symbolic union, the union of opposites, which formed a sacred wholeness – earth and sky, female and male, humanity and divinity.

> The goddess Nammu, whose name is written with the pictograph for 'primeval sea', was the ultimate mother, who gave birth to the cosmic or world mountain. This being had at its base the female Earth known as Ki, and at its summit the male Sky known as An. Ki and An brought forth the air god Enlil,

SUMER

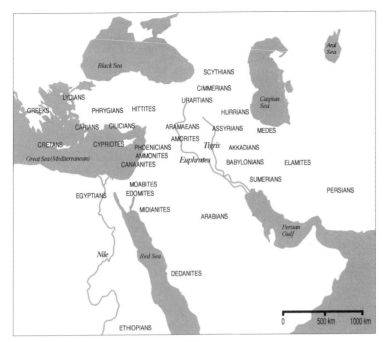

Figure 2: Map of the area from Greece to Persia (Iran) showing the people who occupied the Near East. The three great rivers – Nile, Euphrates and Tigris – made the land they flowed through fertile.

who tore Earth and Sky apart. What was once One – Earth and Sky, female and male – were forced apart.[1]

The forcing apart of Earth and Sky is found in many creation myths. In classical Greek legend Gaia (Earth) and Ouranos (Sky) were separated by their son Kronos. In Egypt the air god Shu separated the world parents, but in this case Sky was female and Earth was male. The New Zealand Maori creation story has Papa, Earth, separated from Rangi, Sky, by their son Tane.

Many ancient cultures had a sacred world mountain, which symbolised the psychic/spiritual union of divinity with humanity. Sumerians built towering replicas of the sacred mountain in many of their cities. These great temples, known as ziggurats, were up to 91 metres tall, approximately 26 storeys in today's terms. They were the cultural and spiritual centres of the civilisation. The most important aspects of a society are still housed today in the tallest buildings. For centuries the tallest buildings in all areas were religious, but today the tallest buildings in Western society are commercial. The destruction of the Twin Towers in New York in 2001 could be seen as a symbolic attack on a sacred structure.

Sumer being a land without stone, ziggurats were made of baked mud brick. They were just as impressive as the stone pyramids, but

See Fig 3, p. 26

THE MYTHS THAT MAKE US

Figure 3: Replica drawing of a late Sumerian ziggurat, c.2050 BCE. Architecturally, ziggurats had tremendous influence on religious structures throughout the world. They may pre-date the first Egyptian pyramid, the step pyramid. Ziggurat-like structures of a much later date can be found east of Sumer, particularly in Central America.

See Figs. 4a (below) and 4b (opposite)

because of the material used they did not have the permanence of the Egyptian structures. Unlike the pyramids, ziggurats had no internal chambers but a lavish accommodation chamber at the top for the gods, goddesses, priests and priestesses. The stairway was for the descent of deities to dwell with humans, and the ascent of humans to divine level (Jacob's dream of a ladder reaching to heaven in Genesis 28 is probably the stairway of a ziggurat). Humanity and divinity were close in Sumerian beliefs. The Old Testament denigrates Sumerian and Babylonian cities and ziggurats in the story of the Tower of Babel (Genesis 11:1ff.). Despite the biblical pronouncement – 'they left off building the city' – many flourishing cities existed with ziggurats at their centre.

The ancients recognised the necessity of non-duality, the union of opposites – female and male, humanity and divinity – for creation to occur. So important was this union in all the Near East, except Israel, that a sacred marriage was part of the belief structure. A symbolic ritual was annually enacted by a priestess representing the goddess, and the priest-king representing the god – a divine connubium as they had been in the beginning.* In Sumer the ceremony was held in the chamber at the top of the ziggurat in springtime and represented the regeneration of life. The Sumerian language had the same word for semen and water, both possessing an engendering power which brings about fertility. Just as man fertilised woman with semen, so the Sky Father fertilised Mother Earth with rain. Many poems written to celebrate this sacred marriage expressed the wonder and delight of the ritual:

> The Earth was arrayed luxuriantly in plants and herbs, its
>   presence was majestic,
> The holy Earth, the pure Earth, beautified herself for holy
>   Heaven,
> Heaven, the noble god, inserted his sex into the wide
>   Earth.[2]

Besides expressing the holiness of Earth, symbolically the ritual was healing the separation, recreating Unity, the union of opposites

---

* Rituals may appear bizarre to the uninitiated. The Romans accused early Christians of cannibalism because of the ritual of drinking the blood and eating the body of Jesus. They also thought Christians were promoting homosexuality because of their talk of 'brotherly love'.

as represented, for example, by the Chinese yin-yang symbol. The concept of union has largely been absent from, and indeed denied, in our culture, but sometimes it appears as in fairy tales such as *Cinderella*, *Snow White* and *The Sleeping Beauty*, where healing, regeneration and harmony are symbolised by the union of female and male. Not only is the 'passive' female made whole by the male, but the 'active' male is made whole by the female, and they live happily ever after. The historian of religions Mircea Eliade writes:

> ... the One, the Unity, the Totality were desires revealed in myths and beliefs and expressed in rites and mystical techniques. On the level of presystematic thought, the mystery of totality embodies man's endeavour to reach a perspective in which the contraries are abolished ... The fact that these archaic themes and motifs still survive in folklore and continually arise in the worlds of dreams and imagination proves that the mystery of totality forms an integral part of the human drama. It recurs under various aspects and at all levels of cultural life – in mystical philosophy and theology, in the mythologies and folklore of the world, in modern men's dreams and fantasies and in artistic creation.[3]

Western religions are based on duality not unity, and this leads to the denigration of the opposite by the one with the most power. For example, the Old Testament, centred in Canaan where a goddess culture existed, tells of repeated attempts to destroy the 'abomination' of the female goddess, her sacred groves and trees, and her 'loathsome' practices. The Hebrews saw no divinity in a goddess and what she represented – Earth and Nature. Divinity was seen in her opposite

See Fig. 5, p. 28

Figure 4a (opposite page, bottom): The Warka Vase, c. 3000 BCE, Urak, Sumer (Iraq). At the top of this alabaster vase a royal attendant holds up the king's ceremonial belt. The king, representing the priest/god, is approaching the priestess/goddess's chamber at the top of the ziggurat for an enactment of the sacred marriage. The second level has naked temple servants bearing gifts for the priestess. The bottom three levels have healthy animals and luxuriant plants beside a river or canal.
National Museum of Iraq, Baghdad

Figure 4b (below): The Sacred Marriage, Tell Asmar, Iraq. Sumerian cylinder seal, early 3rd millennium BCE. Joseph Campbell calls this seal 'Marriage of Heaven and Earth' in his book 'The Mythic Image' (p. 82).
Oriental Institute of the University of Chicago

THE MYTHS THAT MAKE US

Figure 5: The Eastern symbol of yin and yang is thought to date back to 3000 BCE in China. Yin is conceived as earth, female, dark, passive and absorbing. Yang is conceived as heaven, male, light, active and penetrating. When in harmony they are depicted as equal light and dark halves of a whole.

only, the far away Yahweh and Heaven, and the goddess culture was to be destroyed, not integrated. This predisposition to denigrate and destroy opposites has had profound effects on Western culture, where differences and distinctions have been highlighted and considered unworthy of respect and reconciliation. Such an attitude has often produced candidates for domination, and led to violence and destruction. Yet there are thinkers in the West who have recognised the importance of the union of opposites to create individual and collective wholeness – for example, Mircea Eliade, Carl Jung, and the physicist David Bohm, who writes:

> The widespread and pervasive distinction between people (race, nation, family, profession, etc. [add to this gender and religion]) … is now preventing mankind from working together for the common good, and indeed, even for survival. … Even if [man] does try to consider the needs of mankind he tends to regard humanity as separate from nature, and so on. What I am proposing is that man's general way of thinking of the totality, ie. his general world view, is crucial for the overall order of the human mind itself. If he thinks of the totality as constituted of independent fragments, then that is how his mind will tend to operate, but if he can include everything coherently and harmoniously in an overall whole that is undivided, unbroken, and without a border (for every border is a division or break) then his mind will tend to move in a similar way, and from this will flow an orderly action within the whole.[4]

CREATION FROM THE FEMALE

Once female and male had been separated they had to come together for creation. *Eridu Genesis* continues:

See Fig. 6, p. 29

> Creation occurred with the union of Ki and Enlil, beginning with the water god of vegetation and wisdom, Enki. Other gods and goddesses were created and they lived much as humans did on earth, tilling fields of grain. The god of the Sky, An, stood alone and all knowing in the sky. He was an impartial judge and respected for his justice. He was also the

keeper of the bread and water of eternal life that made the gods immortal.

There came a time when the crops failed due to neglect by the tending gods and goddesses. Nammu, the great water grand-dam, seeing the plight of her progeny, asked Enki, the cleverest of all the gods and goddesses, to make servants so they would do the work for the deities. Enki agreed, instructing his grandmother to take clay from the bottom of the Earth and to shape it to form heart and limbs. Enki's wife, the important Earth-goddess Ninhursag gave birth, with eight goddesses of birth to assist. 'The Earth-mother will have fixed the image of gods upon it.' And so it was done. The gods and goddesses were delighted with Enki who had invented humans to serve them as slaves.[5]

Figure 6: Drawing from an Akkadian cylinder seal, 2300–2233 BCE. Enki, the god of sweet waters, is climbing the sacred mountain (ziggurat). From his shoulders spring the Euphrates and Tigris rivers. He holds the thunderbird, signifying clouds rising from the waters, and the animal at his feet is an ibex, symbol of underground springs.

This multi-layered creation myth affected all Sumerian society. It was a story woven around beliefs stretching back hundreds of years.

In the early agricultural societies, before civilisations developed, the female was highly venerated. Thousands of female figurines have been found by archaeologists particularly in Asia Minor and the Near East. They are small enough to be held in the hand, making them very personal. Some have pointed ends so they could be stuck in the ground. Early ones have enlarged buttocks and marked pubic areas symbolising the sanctity of female creation. Male figurines have also been found but fewer in number. It is thought that whilst the masculine was recognised as part of the creative and sustaining force, the feminine was all-embracing, at the heart of creation and the life principle. The mythologist Joseph Campbell writes:

> ... the focal figure of all mythology and worship was the bountiful goddess Earth, as the mother and nourisher of life and receiver of the dead for rebirth. In the earliest period of her cult (perhaps c. 7500–3500 BC in the Levant [eastern Mediterranean]) such a mother-goddess may have been thought of only as a local patroness of fertility, as many anthropologists suppose. However, in the temples even of the first of the higher civilisations (Sumer, c. 3500–2350 BC), the Great Goddess of highest concern was certainly much more than that. She was ... the substance of their bodies, configurator of their lives and thoughts, and receiver of their dead.[6]

Men and women were created from the goddess's body, sustained by another form of her body (plants and animals as food), and returned to her body in death. The Mother Goddess, Earth, was alive; therefore, to die and be buried within her was to take part in another form of her life. Time was cyclical, the phases of the moon, the round of the seasons and the rotation of the constellations proceeding in an endless cycle – and such was the form of human life too. One can imagine that death would no longer be feared if it involved the physical return to the original, nurturing Mother from whence we came, to become another form of her divinity. The terms 'Mother Earth' and 'Mother Nature' have survived from antiquity, demonstrating the powerful force and archetype she has remained despite efforts to get rid of her.

Eridu Genesis expressed this theme of human divinity with the ultimate mother, Nammu, being the creatrix and her daughter Ki being Earth; humans were shaped from Ki's body by Nammu, and physically born of the goddess Ninhursag. All humans carried divinity within them, being fashioned, formed and born of goddesses. A culture that honours women in its creation will also honour them in its laws and customs. The historian Donald Mackenzie lists some examples of women's high social status in early civilisations:

See Fig. 7, p. 31

> The Ancient Sumerians ... like the Mediterranean peoples of Egypt and Crete, reverenced and exalted motherhood in social and religious life. Women were accorded a legal status and marriage laws were promulgated by the State. Wives could possess private property in their own right, as did the Babylonian Sarah, wife of Abraham, who owned the Egyptian slave Hagar [Genesis 16:1ff.]. A woman received from her parents a marriage dowry, and in the event of separation from her husband could claim its full value back from her husband... Brothers and sisters were joint heirs of the family estate. Dungi II, an early Sumerian king, appointed two of his daughters as rulers of conquered cities in Syria and Elam. Similarly Shishak, the Egyptian Pharaoh, handed over the city of Gezer, which he had subdued, to his daughter, Solomon's wife [1 Kings 9:16]. In religious life the female population exercised an undoubted influence, and in certain temples there were priestesses.[7]

SACRED SYMBOLS

The creative arts of a culture – music, literature, stories, poems and the visual arts – express some of the important elements of that culture. So it is with Sumer, as seen in the Warka Vase and the beautiful Warka Head. The sacred was so much part of life in ancient times it was central to all artwork. The power of the god of fresh water was in the water, the power of the goddess of wild animals was in the animals.

Because the beliefs of different ancient cultures were similar, they

Figure 7: The white marble Warka Head, c. 3000 BCE, found in the Temple Precinct, Urak, Sumer. A portrait of a priestess/goddess. The eyebrows and eyes would have been inlaid with lapis lazuli and hair would have been fitted.
National Museum of Iraq, Baghdad

THE MYTHS THAT MAKE US

were understood, accepted and accommodated across borders. Sumer engaged in extensive foreign trade and Sumerian ideas as well as written language and goods travelled along the trade routes to Crete, and from there it is believed to Greece.

Serpents were often depicted with deities, particularly goddesses. Symbols of healing, wisdom and immortality, they were venerated in many cultures over many centuries – but as with the sacred marriage, not in Israel. The serpent suffered drastically in the Western interpretation of Genesis. Its wisdom became 'crafty' or 'subtle'. Wisdom in Greek was *sophia*, as in our word 'philosophy', love of wisdom. The word *sophia* had a practical meaning, referring originally to the craft of handling things. The word 'crafty' has come to mean cunning, but originally it referred to wisdom, creative ability.

See Fig. 8, below

In Genesis the serpent's knowledge of immortality was displayed by its informing Eve 'You will not die'. It was the first to be cursed by Yahweh – 'Because you have done this, cursed are you above all cattle, and above all wild animals.' It was also separated from its

Figure 8: Ivory carvings of Asclepius, god of healing and his wife or daughter, Hygieia, goddess of health, late 4th century CE, Rome. Our word 'hygiene' comes from the goddess's name, and the modern caduceus of the medical profession is taken from Asclepius's emblem of a serpent coiled around a staff – the symbol of healing. The cult of Asclepius believed that healing occurred through dreams, pre-dating the dream connection theories of Carl Jung by nearly 2000 years.
National Museums Liverpool

ancient connection with the female – 'I will put enmity between you and the woman' (Genesis 3:4ff.). Yet it maintained its power to heal in Numbers 21:8ff. – 'And the Lord said to Moses, "Make a fiery serpent, and set it on a pole; and every one who is bitten [by a snake] when he sees it, shall live".'

Closely associated with the goddess and her wise serpent in ancient myths was the Tree of Life. Sacred trees were planted in temple grounds throughout the Near East, Egypt, Crete and Greece – but not in Israel. These trees represented the union of Earth and Heaven. The roots were embedded in Earth and reached up to Heaven to form a union with divinity in the same way as ziggurats. Humans were encouraged to eat from these trees, gaining the wisdom that the powerful cycle of life was eternal. Modern-day physics tells us that matter and energy can be neither created nor destroyed, each is a different form of the other. Trees in ancient beliefs had the spirit of deities within them, and when the trees bore fruit, humans were invited to pick and eat that life-sustaining force as gifts from the gods and goddesses.

It is a completely different story in Genesis where another tree is introduced, the tree of knowledge. This knowledge is the knowledge of opposites – God and humanity, Heaven and Earth, life and death, man and woman, good and evil, right and wrong. Eating from this tree would be punished by exclusion from the Garden of Eden, and exclusion from the unifying force of the tree of life where all living things are One and opposites are eliminated. 'And the Lord God

Figure 9: Cylinder seal, c. 2200 BCE. Seated goddess and god (deities were usually depicted seated) with their attendant serpents, gesture invitingly to the date palm's fruit. Joseph Campbell calls this seal 'The Tree of Life' in his book The Mythic Image *(p. 295).*
British Museum, London

See Fig. 9, above

commanded the man, saying, "You may freely eat of every tree of the garden; but of the tree of knowledge of good and evil you shall not eat, for in the day that you eat of it you shall die"' (Genesis 2:16ff.). The punishment for eating from that tree was banishment from the Garden, 'with the cherubim, and a flaming sword which turned every way, to guard the way to the tree of life' (Genesis 3:24) – that sacred tree. The theme of something forbidden ('Thou shalt not') is a widespread motif in fairy tales, for example the forbidden room in Bluebeard. Generally the forbidding figure flies into a rage when he is disobeyed, as in Genesis.[8]

With today's psychological knowledge, the Garden of Eden story could be interpreted differently: eating the fruit from the tree of knowledge could be taken to symbolise the birth of consciousness in humanity, initiated by the woman, Eve, guided by the serpent, Wisdom. Or eating from the tree of knowledge could be symbolically part of the development leading from an all-embracing, innocent childhood, Paradise, to the awakening of separate self-consciousness – learning to fit into a society that dictates what is 'good' and what is 'evil'. How different Western society might have been if one of these interpretations had been applied.

The eradication of anything to do with a goddess and her sacred symbols continued throughout the patriarchal history of the Old Testament. About 621 BCE the king of Judah, Josiah, set about eliminating all such pagan beliefs.

> And the king defiled the high places that were east of Jerusalem, to the south of the mount of corruption, which Solomon the king of Israel had built [300 years earlier] for Ashoreth the abomination of the Sidonians ... and cut down the Asherim [trees] and filled their places with the bones of men.

But despite the destruction and zeal of Josiah,

> Still the Lord did not turn from the fierceness of his great wrath, by which his anger was kindled against Judah, because of the provocations with which Manasseh [a previous king who had allowed pagan ways] had provoked him. (2 Kings 23:13ff.)

All this is very different from the tolerant mother goddess.

SUMERIAN STORIES IN THE OLD TESTAMENT

Despite the antipathy of the Hebrews to surrounding pagan religions, they borrowed many stories from the ancient myths of Sumer for their own historical myth. An, the God who stood alone and all-knowing in the sky in *Eridu Genesis*, appears to be a precursor of Yahweh. But An was an impartial judge, whereas Yahweh's judgements were exclusively partial to the Hebrews.

The biblical story of Adam being put in the Garden of Eden 'to till it and keep it' (Genesis 2:15) is similar to the earlier story in *Eridu Genesis* of humans being created to do the deities' work of tilling the fields.

The competition between farming and sheep herding for the favour of a deity – Cain and Abel in Genesis 4 – has a different slant when told by the peace-loving Sumerians:

> The farmer Enkimdu [Cain] and the shepherd Dumuzi [Abel] vied for the goddess Inanna's favours, hoping to marry her. Inanna appeared to prefer Enkimdu, 'the farmer who makes plants grow abundantly.' Dumuzi then gave a long list of qualities that showed his produce to be superior to those of Enkimdu, and tried to pick a quarrel with the farmer. Enkimdu refused to enter into a quarrel, responding by peaceably offering the shepherd grazing rights: 'In my meadowland let thy sheep walk about.' There was eventually a marriage and the unsuccessful suitor was invited.[9]

The Sumerian story is one of peace and reconciliation, ending with a marriage, a union of female and male so symbolic to Sumerians. The Genesis story is one of envy, anger, murder and punishment, with Cain killing his younger brother Abel when Yahweh favours Abel's gift of 'the firstlings of his flock'. Cain, the farmer, was cursed and banished from his land by Yahweh. Abel, the younger, favoured brother, was a shepherd and the early Hebrews were shepherds. Effectively the biblical story is a character assassination of settled farmers whose land the Hebrews wanted to roam with their animals. The Sumerian story is more like a Jesus saying 'Love your enemy' or 'Turn the other cheek' rather than anything in Old Testament history, which is markedly lacking in the balancing female influence. In a story without any feminine element the unconscious attributes of the 'loving' way in which people relate to one another is absent. This can be said of Yahweh – 'passionately partisan, [with] little compassion for anyone but his own favourites ... simply a tribal deity'.[10]

The Hebrews borrowed the Great Flood story from Sumer, a land that was subject to sudden and devastating floods from its two great rivers. But there are subtle differences between the Sumerian and biblical stories. Genesis tells us that

> The Lord saw that the wickedness of man was great in the earth, and that every imagination of the thoughts of his heart was only evil continually. And the Lord was sorry that he had made man on the earth, and it grieved him to his heart. So the Lord said, 'I will blot out man whom I have created from the face of the ground, man and beast and creeping things and birds of the air, for I am sorry I have made them.' But Noah found favour in the eyes of the Lord. (Genesis 6:5ff.)

In the earlier Sumerian flood story, however, it is different, with the compassion of a goddess present:

> The gods, annoyed by the noise created by humans decided to destroy them by sending a flood. 'The holy Inanna lamented on account of her people.' Enki revealed the deities' plan to Ziusudra, an obedient and humble man, and the god told him to build a large boat. This Ziusudra did and successfully rode the flood.[11]

In the Sumerian version there is the compassion of the goddess and no mention of humanity's evil, although they did upset the deities with their noise. This may be a reference to the fact that cities were expanding rapidly and perhaps even becoming overpopulated as people crowded into their walled protection, creating more hustle and bustle. The Sumerologist Thorkild Jacobsen explains:

> As far as we can judge, the fourth millennium and the ages before it had been moderately peaceful. Wars and raids were not unknown; but they were not constant and they did not dominate existence. In the third millennium they appear

to have become the order of the day. No one was safe. The quickness with which an enemy could strike – some warlord bound for loot to fill the long boats in which he moved along the network of major canals … made life, even for the wealthy and powerful, uncertain and insecure.[12]

The Akkadian leader Sargon invaded Sumer about 2334 BCE. He became the first empire-builder, uniting the city-states, and creating a model government that influenced all surrounding civilisation. He built on the trade already established and commercial connections flourished. His beginnings became legend:

> My mother, an enitum [temple priestess] conceived me; in secret she bore me,
> She set me in a basket of rushes, with bitumen she sealed my lid,
> She cast me into the river, which rose not over me,
> The river bore me up and carried me to Akki, the drawer of water.
> Akki, the drawer of water, lifted me out as he dipped his bucket.
> Akki, the drawer of water, took me as his son and reared me,
> Akki, the drawer of water, appointed me as his gardener.
> While I was a gardener, Ishtar [the Goddess] granted me love,
> And for four and … years I exercised kingship,
> The black-headed people [Sumerians] I ruled, I governed.[13]

This was a thousand years before Moses was born, but the similarities in Exodus 2 cannot be missed. Joseph Campbell argues that the story of Moses cannot have originated in Egypt as that country did not have the knowledge of bitumen at that time. Just as Moses led his people to 'the land of milk and honey' that was Canaan, so Sargon lead his people into the land of milk and honey that was Sumer. Though they affected the culture, they assimilated much of it, creating an even richer civilisation.

Abraham, the Hebrew patriarch revered by the three great monotheistic religions – Judaism, Christianity and Islam – lived in the Sumerian city of Ur. Since he did not leave Sumer for Canaan until about 2000

BCE, he would have seen ziggurats and heard the sacred stories told. No doubt he carried these memories with him and told the stories, to be retold by succeeding generations. Eventually these memories and stories were adapted to the requirements of the emerging Hebrews. To bond the separate Hebrew tribes together into a cohesive, conquering group that could justifiably overrun a superior goddess culture required a different belief system. A new creation myth was needed, and the known Sumerian stories were altered to fit the new order. The process of defaming the existing goddess beliefs and terming them evil also occurred. Joseph Campbell calls this occurrence 'mythical defamation':

> It consists simply in terming the gods of other people demons ... and then inventing all sorts of both great and little secondary myths to illustrate, on the one hand, the impotence and malice of the demons and, on the other, the majesty and righteousness of the great god or gods. It is used ... to validate in mythological terms not only a new social order but also a new psychology ...[14]

The Hebrews did this most successfully to the surrounding goddess religions, creating an 'us and them' dichotomy. But we should not think the process of mythical defamation is an archaic phenomenon – it happened during the Crusades and still happens today. We find it wherever people of different religions, politics, classes and races are said, or believed, to be inherently evil: for example, Hitler against the Jews, McCarthyism in the USA in the early 1950s, and George W. Bush's talk of 'the Axis of Evil'.

SUMER'S HISTORY

Sumer with its wealth was seen as a highly prized jewel by outsiders, be they individual raiding warlords or more organised invaders. Amongst the latter were the Elamites from the east (c. 2500 BCE), Sargon's Akkadians from the north (c. 2334 BCE), the semi-barbaric Gutians from the mountains (c. 2230 BCE), and the Amorites from the north-west (c. 2000 BCE). All these warrior aggressors brought with them their own cultures, which were less developed than the Sumerian. In many ways the Sumerian culture conquered

SUMER

Figure 10: The Stele of Hammurabi with the laws written in cuneiform around it, c. 1730 BCE. On the upper part, seated at the summit of the World Mountain, is the sun god, Shamash, god of righteousness and law. He is handing Hammurabi a stylus with which to write the legal code. Hammurabi salutes with his right hand raised. This is very similar to Moses going 'up the mountain of God', Mt Sinai, some 500 years later, and receiving the Law from God (Exodus 19ff.). But the laws of Hammurabi and the Law of Moses are very different. Hammurabi's laws were for a long-established, sophisticated culture. The Law of Moses was for a band of primitive tribes wandering in the desert. Inscribed on the stele are 282 case laws, covering economic provisions (prices, tariffs, trade and commerce), family law (marriage, divorce), criminal law (assault, theft) and civil law (slavery, debt).
Musée du Louvre, Paris

the invaders, but changes were inevitable.

This occurred most notably with Hammurabi, an Amorite who ruled over Sumer from 1792 to 1750 BCE. He promulgated a Code of Laws, built on the body of Sumerian law that had existed for centuries. Donald Mackenzie calls this Code 'a curious blending of the principles of "Father right" and "Mother right"' – the patriarchal culture of the invaders and the goddess culture of the Sumerians. In fact, as Mackenzie points out, ancient Sumerian respect for women still existed during the time of Hammurabi:

See Fig. 10, above

Vestal virgins and married women were protected against the slanderer. Any man who 'pointed the finger' against them unjustifiably was charged with the offence before a judge, who sentenced him to have his forehead branded. It was not difficult, therefore, in ancient Babylonia to discover the men who made malicious and unfounded statements regarding an innocent woman.[15]

The Amorites made Babylon their capital and this city became the political and commercial centre of the Tigris-Euphrates area. Science and scholarship flourished in the great Babylonian empire created by uniting Sumer, Akkadia and part of Assyria to the north. Ruling this empire and protecting it from outsiders became the order of the day. To do this a collective attitude towards defence and aggression was required. The most effective way of cementing a collective attitude is to have it symbolically presented within the sanctity of a creation myth. The rituals and collective psyche of wholeness and peace that arose from *Eridu Genesis* were useless for stimulating the aggressive values deemed necessary, and so a new creation myth was required by the empire of Babylonia.

BABYLONIA

The creation myth *Enuma Elish* set Babylonian values and influenced all Near Eastern cultures. The first mention we have of this powerful story is from a tablet dated 1580 BCE, but the myth itself dates from much earlier.

Enuma Elish

In the beginning there was just the watery abyss, Apsu, the sweet waters of the underground, and Tiamat, the sea. They mingled their waters together and in their mingling the first gods came into being. Generation followed generation.

These gods enjoyed dancing, surging back and forth, so upsetting their great grandam, Tiamat. Apsu finally had had enough and wanted to destroy the gods but Tiamat did not want her offspring hurt. Ea [Enki], the youngest and cleverest of the gods heard of Apsu's plan of destruction, killed him and built a temple over his body.

In this temple the god Marduk was born. He was the darling of his grandfather, Anu [An], the god of heaven, who gave his grandson the four winds to play with. Marduk played with these winds stirring up Tiamat again. Finally, the other gods who shared her desire for rest roused her to resistance. She created a mighty army with a spearhead of monsters to destroy the gods and placed Kingu, her consort, at its head.

There was consternation when the other gods heard of this. Eventually young Marduk was approached to fight, which he agreed to do as long as he had absolute authority.

In the following encounter Kingu and his army fled when they saw Marduk. Tiamat, in the form of a monster, serpent or dragon, stood her ground, furious, and was killed by Marduk. He took Kingu and the gods who sided with him captive.

See Fig. 11, p. 43

Marduk then cleaved the body of Tiamat, raising half of her to form heaven and the other half becoming earth. The gods were overjoyed and reaffirmed their allegiance to him

Figure 11: Marduk slaying Tiamat, Assyrian relief (later called Ninurta and the Demon) c. 9th century BCE.
British Museum, London

with the formula 'benefits and obedience'.

Marduk then announced his wish to build the great city Babylon for himself. He pardoned the gods who had sided with Tiamat and set them to building the city. They were so grateful at being let off so lightly they prostrated themselves before 'The King'. Pleased with their homage Marduk wished to release them from the chore of building and planned to create humans to toil for them. On the advice of Ea he had Kingu indicted and executed, and from his blood Ea created humans to do the work.[1]

There was a gigantic shift in this creation myth. The Great Mother, the creatrix, became a monster and was killed. War became legitimate as a means of protecting and furthering one's perceived rights. The Warrior God, the Hero King, saviour and protector, came into being. In one broad stroke the Sumerian unity and peace were swept aside. Marduk became the national god who demanded obedience and granted benefits – an even closer precursor of Yahweh than An had been. *Enuma Elish* was recited and enacted at the religious spring festival for over a thousand years, replacing the symbolic union of the sacred marriage. Thorkild Jacobsen writes:

> The impact of the new ruler concept on contemporary thought can hardly be overestimated. In art the old ritual motifs receded before representations of war and victory; in literature a new form, the epic tale, took its place beside the myth. ... The ruler metaphor – like the ruler concept – could not be lifted out of the social and political context from which it derived its meaning.[2]

THE DEAD MOTHER GODDESS

Marduk killed Tiamat, the Great Mother, 'she who fashions all things' and harbours the body after death. She became a monster and dragon, a power of destruction. Here we have the first step away from the balance of 'wholeness', yin and yang, towards irreconcilable differences, which will culminate in the exclusive 'rightness' of the monotheistic patriarchy. Joseph Campbell comments:

> [*Enuma Elish*] is a forthright patriarchal document, where the female principle is devalued, together with its point of view, and, as always happens when a power of nature and the psyche is excluded from its place, it has turned into its negative, as a demoness, dangerous and fierce.[3]

But the archetype of the Great Mother Goddess did not die. For, as Jung commented, it lives on in the collective unconscious, the soul:

> What, with us, crops up only in dreams and fantasies was once either conscious custom or general belief. But what was once strong enough to mould the spiritual life of a highly developed people will not have vanished without a trace from the human soul ...[4]

According to Plato and Jung the soul is female: it is the powerful female principle that harbours divinity. She is the neglected Great Mother Goddess: the store of memories, place of wisdom, seat of emotions, intuitions and instincts, house of dreams and source of creativity. In dreams, images and creative arts she communicates in age-old archetypes. She is the aspect of ourselves which, Jung believed, modern humanity is seeking to become Whole.

The archetype of the dragon, the winged serpent, was carried into Christendom as symbolic of sin and paganism. It was often depicted prostrate under the heels of saints and martyrs with a maiden to be rescued, as for example in the images of St George slaying the dragon. This maiden is the treasure of inner wisdom in the soul, the benign aspect of the once-respected dragon, understood and released into consciousness. In fairy tales dragons are often depicted as frogs – a male frog for a heroine and a female frog for a hero, as for example in the fairy tales *The Frog Prince* and *The Three Feathers*. In these tales what was deemed ugly and repulsive proves to be handsome and beautiful when respected. The frogs become just what the hero or heroine was looking for to make them whole, and a marriage takes place.

Recently the dragon has emerged from its cloud in the West, as in the movie *Dragonheart* (1996), where it is male, a benevolent trickster who teams up with the hero dragon-hunter to fight the violent tyrant. And in *Shrek* (2001) – which is full of symbolic twists and turns based on many fairy tales, legends, myths and historical events, bound together by a broad understanding of psychology – the reluctant hero is an uncouth ogre motivated by self-interest. (Heroes are usually motivated by rewards, the two most common being fame and fortune, and they have to have an 'enemy' to prove themselves against.) The ferocious dragon guarding the beautiful princess turns out to be a loving female, and the princess and the ogre are more similar than one may have expected – a perfect match.

It is no accident that the archetype of the dragon/monster is being revived in a positive light at the same time as traditional Christianity is failing. These modern-day stories come at a time when the Genesis creation myth with its 'evil' serpent (dragon) is being questioned and repudiated. Western society is increasingly ready to counteract the horror in the Old Testament and our history with other stories. Peace and love are often spoken about by religions, but in reality peace and love can be swept aside quickly and easily by those who wish to maintain or acquire control. But nowadays there is more and more questioning of this kind of control in society.

Traditional religious values have changed little since the time of Marduk. He entered the psyche at a time of invasion and civil wars that caused upheavals and sometimes devastation in Babylonia. The division of 'us' and 'them' came into being, with Marduk protecting the 'us', instilling an attitude that has been inherited in Abrahamic religions.

DIVINITY WITHIN

Despite the change to a powerful creator god in *Enuma Elish* the pantheon of deities continued to exist. A polytheistic culture by its very nature is tolerant – there is always room for another deity in a family of deities, and the deities are not jealous like the Hebrew Yahweh. Individuals can choose which goddess or god they wish to make their own – or perhaps the deity chooses them – to become their personal deity, an immortal daemon who will support and guide them along their path.

In his book *The Treasures of Darkness*, Thorkild Jacobsen describes the original concept of a personal deity. That deity, he writes, be it goddess or god, was taken to dwell in the person's body. If the deity removed itself from the body then 'the body was open for evil demons of disease to take over and "possess" the man'.[5] A few thousand years later Carl Jung reintroduced this ancient belief when he wrote about the private daemon that counsels and whose mandates must be obeyed. If ignored then it will become a demon and cause physical and psychological problems.

Jacobsen goes on to say that the personal goddess or god was taken to pass from the body of the father into the body of his offspring, from generation to generation. Hence the phrase 'The Lord, the God of your fathers, the God of Abraham, the God of Isaac, and the God of Jacob' (Exodus 3:15).[6] From this we understand that Abraham brought such a personal deity from Sumer and it was handed on to his succeeding generations. (Interestingly, in the Old Testament the word 'god' may also mean 'goddess'.) At some time this personal deity was removed, perhaps by Moses, *from the inside to the outside* and became the sole, exclusive God – the Father God of the Hebrew nation. This is the story of the Old Testament. Jesus tried to change that. When he implied that he was Son of God he placed the long-lost inner divinity *within himself*, and tried to teach everybody to do the same by extolling them to find the kingdom of God within. This was radical stuff at that time – a blasphemy of paganism punishable by stoning.

BABYLONIA

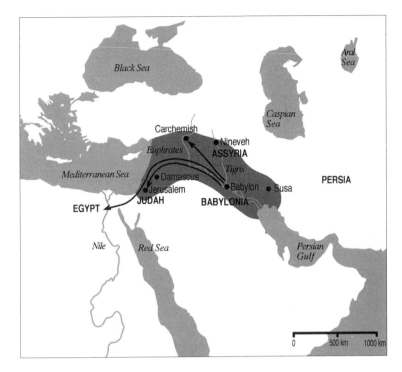

Figure 12: The Babylonian Empire.

Jesus was very careful and never used the term 'inner divinity' directly, but did use the term 'son of the Father' frequently. It was Paul, writing about twenty years after Jesus' crucifixion, who stated that Jesus was exclusively 'designated Son of God in power according to the Spirit of holiness by his resurrection from the dead' (Romans 1:3ff.). It was in this way that the divinity of Jesus came to Christianity, but this is not what Jesus taught. Knowing and appreciating the divinity within is what Jesus wanted people to understand.

BABYLONIAN HISTORY

In 605 BCE Babylonia entered Judaic history when Nebuchadnezzar II, a Chaldean (southern Babylonian), ascended the throne. He was known for his military might, the splendour of his capital Babylon (all in the name of Marduk), and his important part in Jewish history. Nebuchadnezzar consciously pursued a policy of expansion, even attempting to invade Egypt. He captured Jerusalem, destroyed the temple built by Solomon in 957 BCE, and deported many Jews to Babylon in 586 and 582 (2 Chronicles 36:5ff.).

The Persians under Cyrus the Great captured Babylonia in 539

See Fig. 12, above

BCE. Cyrus gave the captive Jews permission to return to Israel and assisted them in rebuilding the Jerusalem Temple. Two-thirds of the Jews chose to remain in the beautiful, thriving, liberal city of Babylon, and so became the first Jewish community to live permanently in diaspora. Many of the later books of the Old Testament were written in Babylon.

Babylonia never became independent after Cyrus, eventually passing in 331 BCE to the Macedonian leader, Alexander the Great. Alexander, who claimed to be descended from the gods, was impressed by the Babylonian wisdom and accomplishments and added Marduk to his pantheon. He planned to make the magnificent city of Babylon the capital of his empire, but he died aged 33 in 323 BCE. The Greeks eventually left, and much of the knowledge and wisdom of ancient Sumer faded.

The shift from a great mother creatrix to a protective male creator had happened, setting the stage for another shift to occur: the entrance of an omnipotent deity, the transcendent, jealous male creator-god who promises exclusive benefits to all who obey his commands.

ABRAHAM AND HIS DESCENDANTS

The Genesis creation myth was probably not put into written form until the reign of King David, about 950 BCE. In this myth, all the magical, mysterious divinity in heaven and earth was attributed exclusively to the male creator, Yahweh.

The first eleven chapters of Genesis narrate the primeval history of the world, and appear to borrow extensively from Sumerian stories – for example, rivalry between farmer and shepherd for the favour of a deity (Cain and Abel), the Flood, and the defamation of ziggurats (the Tower of Babel). Abraham left Sumer about 2000 BCE, and so he would have known ancient Sumerian stories, seen ziggurats, and carried within him his personal deity. 'Now the Lord said to Abram, "Go from your country and your kindred and your father's house to the land I will show you. And I will make you a great nation"' (Genesis 12:1). With his wife and family Abraham followed the caravan route via Harran to Hebron in Canaan, today part of the West Bank territory. Hebron is considered a holy city by Jews and Muslims because of Abraham. There he was accepted, and lived peacefully as an alien in a foreign land. Being shepherds the family found and followed pastures for their animals, leading a semi-nomadic life between Canaan and the fertile Nile delta of Egypt.

Sarah, Abraham's wife, could not have children, so she gave her Egyptian slave-girl, Hagar, to Abraham as a concubine. Being a Sumerian or married under Sumerian law Sarah maintained rights over her property, in this case her slave Hagar. Hagar bore a son, Ishmael. Eventually Sarah also had a son, Isaac, and she became jealous of Ishmael. She prevailed upon Abraham to send Hagar and Ishmael into the desert, where God spoke to Hagar '… I will make [Ishmael] a great nation' (Genesis 21:18). It is from this line that Mohammed, the founder of Islam, held that the faith he proclaimed was the pristine religion of Abraham through Ishmael, the ancestor of the Arabs.

Isaac became known as Israel, the ancestor of the people of Israel. His son Jacob and family migrated to Egypt at a time of famine. They remained there for generations, becoming known as Hebrews. The origin of that word is uncertain. One hypothesis is that it comes from *Habiru* – a class of semi-nomadic people who made their living by hiring themselves out for various services and who eventually became enslaved, providing manpower for the massive building projects of the pharoahs.

MOSES

Moses, a hero figure, led the Hebrews out of Egypt in the 13th century BCE (Exodus 2ff.). Classical heroes/saviours in myth and legend, like Moses, have a common background. They are secretly of high birth, with noble, priestly or divine parentage, threatened at an early age, brought up in humble circumstances and come to power later in life.[1] Other figures who have such legendary beginnings are Sargon of Sumer, the Persian religious reformer Zoroaster, the Persian conqueror Cyrus the Great, and Jesus.

Moses at first glance appears to be of lowly birth – a Hebrew slave's child put into a basket which floated down a river, until found by Pharaoh's daughter. But note the similarity to Sargon's story: just as Sargon's mother was a priestess, so Moses' parents were of the tribe of Levi who were later to have sole rights as servants of the Temple. Having such parentage gave him a much higher rank in Hebrew eyes than being brought up as a member of Egyptian royalty.

Moses killed an Egyptian he saw beating a Hebrew, then fled into the Arabian Desert. There he lived with the Midianites who were descended from Abraham and his second wife, Keturah. The Midianites were a nomadic tribe engaged in pastoral pursuits, caravan trading and banditry. Whilst living there Moses worked as a shepherd, and married Zipporah, the daughter of Jethro the priest-leader of the Kenite sub-tribe. It has been speculated that Yahweh was a Midianite god, and Moses learnt about him from them. Certainly Moses had his first encounter with Yahweh whilst there, 'keeping the flock of his father-in-law, Jethro, the priest of Midian' (Exodus 3). After Moses had led the Hebrews out of Egypt Jethro visited them, and on hearing what Yahweh had done he commented: 'Now I know that the Lord is greater than all gods.' From this statement Yahweh appears to be head of a pantheon. It was Jethro who then officiated at a sacrifice to Yahweh, and advised Moses about setting up the

Hebrew judiciary (Exodus 18).

The freedom of the Hebrews and their exodus from Egypt had not been easy – Yahweh made it that way. He said, 'I will harden [Pharaoh's] heart, so he will not let the people go' (Exodus 4:21ff.). And so Yahweh poisoned the Nile, sent plagues of frogs, gnats, flies, and locusts, dust that caused boils, a devastating hailstorm, and darkness over the land for three days. After inflicting all this suffering on innocent Egyptians, still 'the Lord hardened Pharaoh's heart, and he would not let them go' (Exodus 10:27). Eventually Yahweh killed all the first-born Egyptians, and Pharaoh gave the Hebrews permission to leave.

Historically, about 1500 BCE the island of Thera in the Aegean Sea erupted in one of the largest volcanic eruptions known. Ash and pumice from this eruption have been found in Egypt. Many of the strange happenings recorded in Exodus could be attributed to legendary tales about this eruption and the effects that sulphuric acid and clouds of ash have on humans, animals and the ecology.

Yahweh is presented in this biblical story as a horrific deity. Not only does he bring every type of devastation to the Egyptians, but he causes it by his control over Pharaoh's emotions and actions. There is no compassion of the goddess here, no understanding that all humanity is One. The emphasis has completely shifted to tribal elitism, with the all-powerful Yahweh at the head of the tribe. Suffering, death and destruction come to those who do not have the patronage of Yahweh. Rudolf Otto, a 20th-century German Protestant theologian, terms Yahweh at this stage a '"pre-god" … out of which the "god" gradually grows.'[2] This 'pre-god' has come into the religion as 'The God'. Those who believe these Old Testament stories have this deity at the centre of their belief. As a consequence they may unconsciously emulate this deity in their personal lives, and readily follow a leader who shows these qualities.

From the top of Mt. Sinai, the mountain of God, Moses received the Ten Commandments, the Law and the Covenant (Exodus 19ff.). Their liberation from Egypt laid upon the people the obligation of exclusive loyalty to Yahweh. This meant banning all other deities. The Hebrews were Yahweh's chosen people and he promised them the land of Canaan if they remained faithful to him. Their faithlessness was a constant problem as they often turned away from Yahweh to Baal, the head of the pantheon in Canaan, and the goddess known as Asherah, Anath or Astarte, 'Queen of Heaven'. These pagan deities

See Fig. 13, p. 53

ABRAHAM AND HIS DESCENDANTS

became responsible for all the bad things that happened to the Hebrews: 'When disaster struck Israel ... the fault was found in the regression of the Hebrews to the Canaanite religion.'[3] Its goddesses became associated with evil, and 'righteous' punishment by Yahweh followed transgressions.

In Hebrew society a corresponding denigration of women occurred.

> Woman was regarded as the helpmate rather than the companion and equal of men... A wife had no rights other than those accorded to her by her husband, who exercised over her the power of life and death. Sons inherited family

Figure 13: Gold pendant from northern Canaan, now northern Syria, c. 1400 BCE. A goddess known by many names throughout the Near East – Astarte and Ashtoreth in the Old Testament, Qadishtu in Akkadia, Qedesha, Lady of Kadesh (Syria) in Egypt. She is standing on a lion, with snakes around her body.
Musée du Louvre, Paris

possessions; the daughters had no share allotted to them, and could be sold by fathers and brothers.[4]

Only if a daughter had no brothers could she inherit, and a semblance of this law has survived in the succession of the British monarchy. There is still an element in Western society that favours sons inheriting ahead of daughters. Under Sumerian law daughters inherited equally with sons, a man could leave his property to his wife if he so wished, and women always maintained the right to their dowries, whereas wealth and power were diverted from Hebrew women where possible. This is a good example of the way in which creation myths affect the laws of societies. In their book *The Myth of the Goddess* Ann Baring and Jules Cashford explain:

> It was the idea of Eve's responsibility for the expulsion from the Garden, enshrined in Hebrew text and legend, that became the justification for making Jewish women subject to their fathers and husbands so they no longer possessed even the small degree of sexual, social, political and religious autonomy belonging to women of surrounding cultures… However, it is essential to remember that the myth, and its implications, together with the patriarchal customs regarding women, were *not* endorsed by Jesus – quite the contrary – but they were transmitted from the Old to the New Testament through the writings of Paul, and so they entered formal Christian doctrine.[5]

Creation myths are deeply embedded in societies and their influence is very difficult to eradicate. Psychologically, we could say that the Genesis creation myth and the subsequent laws were based on an unconscious fear of the power of women. As Eve had the power to make Adam eat the forbidden fruit, so woman was to be feared. An example of this fear, and an effective way of segregating women for a week every month, thereby excluding them from public life and leadership, was to declare menstruating women unclean and untouchable. This is done in the Old Testament:

> When a woman has a discharge of blood which is her regular discharge from her body, she shall be in her impurity for seven days, and whoever touches her shall be unclean until

evening. And everything upon which she lies ... sits ... shall be unclean. And whoever touches anything upon which she sits shall wash his clothes, and bathe himself in water, and be unclean until the evening. (Leviticus 15:19ff.)

The regular bleeding of women was regarded with awe: how could anyone bleed like that, then heal themselves? And what is more, this bleeding was somehow connected with the mysterious phases of the moon and the movement of the tides. So it was thought that women must have some power that men did not have, the type of frightening, supernatural power that could affect men. The belief in this frightening female power was still alive at the time the gospels of Mark and Luke were written: when the haemorrhaging woman touched Jesus' cloak he felt 'that power had gone forth from him' (Mark 5:30, Luke 8:45). (The King James Version uses the word 'virtue' instead of 'power'.)*

THE RISE AND FALL OF ISRAEL

Yahweh promised the Hebrews the land of Canaan. Joshua, a charismatic warrior, set about acquiring the land as Moses had instructed: 'You must utterly destroy them; you shall make no covenant with them, and show no mercy to them'. (Deuteronomy 7:2)

> When the Hebrews entered Canaan, they did not find a sparsely populated land with primitive people, but a country with a powerful religion and cultural tradition in which queens took the role of high priestesses, and ordinary women were priestesses. Strong and wealthy cities had long been established in Canaan that had trading connections with Egypt, Babylonia and the Hittite kingdom of Anatolia.[6]

It is now believed that the Hebrew conquest happened gradually over a couple of centuries until the rise of David in the mid-10th century BCE. Until then, for the most part, walled cities remained

---

*In 1611 when the King James version was published, 'virtue' meant 'power'. The Concise Oxford Dictionary and the New Collins Concise English Dictionary have 'inherent power' listed under virtue.

THE MYTHS THAT MAKE US

Figure 14: Gold and ivory statuette of a Snake Goddess, c. 1600 BCE. Though found in Greece it is thought to be from Crete. The bare-breasted goddess – typical of Cretan art – is holding two gold snakes. The piece demonstrates a high level of craftmanship.
Museum of Fine Arts, Boston

in Canaanite hands. Some cities were attacked and razed as in Joshua 6:21ff.: 'They utterly destroyed all in the city, both men and women, young and old, oxen, sheep, and asses, with the edge of the sword… And they burned the city with fire, and all within it… So the lord was with Joshua; and his fame was in all the land.' Barbarous as such acts are, they continue to be perpetrated. For example: the bombing of Dresden in 1945, which virtually destroyed this beautiful city with little or no military advantage; the total destruction of villages during the Vietnam War; pogroms, genocide and ethnic cleansing – the blind destruction of what is not respected, appreciated or understood. Those who believe in the fundamentals of the Old Testament Yahweh may all too easily be incited by a hero leader 'with an ardour of righteous eloquence and a fury of fire and sword'.[7] Carl Jung states:

> The absence of human morality in Yahweh is a stumbling block which cannot be overlooked … We miss reason and moral values, that is two main characteristics of a mature human mind. It is therefore obvious that the Yahwistic image or conception of the deity is less that of certain human specimens: the image of a personified brutal force and of an unethical and non-spiritual mind, yet inconsistent enough to exhibit traits of kindness and generosity beside a violent power-drive. It is the picture of a sort of nature-demon and at the same time of a primitive chieftain aggrandised to a colossal size, just the sort of conception one would expect of a more or less barbarous society. …[8]

The Hebrews did not inhabit the cities of Canaan or make military use of them. Unlike other cultures in the Near East they lacked the experience and level of sophistication required to maintain a complex urban civilisation. Joshua appears to have headed a mobile community moving westward, a force to be reckoned with in the open spaces between the walled cities. Any survivors of the invasion of Canaan were put to forced labour (Judges 1:27ff.). Joshua divided the conquered lands among eleven of the twelve tribes descended from Jacob. The twelfth tribe, the Levites, had religious functions such as guarding the Ark (a wooden coffer in which the Tables of the Law were kept). Tribalism continued.

At approximately the same time that the Hebrews entered Canaan, the Philistines settled on the southern coast. They came from the sophisticated civilisation of the Aegean area, possibly Crete, and may well have been driven out of their island by the eruption of Thera and a later Greek invasion. The gigantic eruption of Thera, only 100 kilometres across the Aegean Sea from Crete, would have caused tsunamis, falling ash, sulphuric acid rain, climate change and crop failure that would have decimated the population, making them vulnerable to attack by the Greeks. The Philistines fled, taking with them the art and craft of their race to the land that became known as Philistia. They established at least five linked city-states along the coast, and then attempted to move into the hill country where the Israelites were. Their knowledge was far superior to that of the Hebrews – 'Now there was no smith to be found throughout all the land of Israel ... but everyone of the Israelites went down to the Philistines to sharpen his plowshare, his mattock, his axe, or his sickle. ... So on the day of battle there was neither sword nor spear found in the hand of any of the people with Saul [the Israelites]' (1 Samuel 13:19ff.). 'Slingers' such as David were acknowledged as specialist warrior marksmen. In Judges 20:16 it is written that the Benjaminites had 'seven hundred picked men who ... could sling a stone at a hair, and not miss'. David was a Benjamite. He only stunned Goliath with the stone he slung: he had to use Goliath's sword to kill him.

See Fig. 14, p. 56

See Fig. 15, below

Excavated Philistine sites have revealed splendid architecture, beautiful jewellery and ornaments, and a distinctive type of pottery. (Little or nothing exists of Hebrew art because of the Second Commandment [Exodus 20:4, Deuteronomy 5:8] – 'You shall not make yourself a graven image, or any likeness of anything that is in heaven above, or that is in the earth beneath, or that is in the water under the earth.') The Philistines have been defamed in the Old Testament, and today the word 'Philistine' means uncultured, but they had one of the most splendid cultures in the ancient world, far superior to that of the Hebrews. The Greeks appreciated the style and grace of the Philistines and named the area Palestine after them.

The Israelites lived in a loose coalition of tribes, but fear of the Philistines eventually united them under a monarch. From 1030 to 920 BCE the kings Saul, David, and Solomon staved off the Philistines. David spent 16 months with them as a mercenary where he learnt much about their superior skills (1 Samuel 27). The one who killed the most was the greatest hero – 'Saul has slain his thousands, and David his ten thousands' (1 Samuel 29:5). In a conflict situation

Figure 15: Stone relief of a slinger, mid-10th century BCE. Aramaen (north-east Syria).
British Museum, London

classical heroes and martyrs – those who die for a cause – are closely associated with unsparing violence.

With Solomon a period of prosperity ensued. He erected a temple in Jerusalem and undertook many other building projects, which burdened the people with heavy taxes and forced labour. He was granted wisdom by Yahweh, who turned against him when Solomon forged peaceful alliances by marrying women 'from the nations concerning which the Lord had said to the people of Israel, "You shall not enter into marriage with them ... for surely they will turn away your heart after their gods".' This they did, 'for Solomon went after Ashtoreth the goddess of the Sidonians' amongst others. 'So Solomon did what was evil in the sight of the Lord ... And the Lord was angry with Solomon' for disobeying his commands, saying 'I will surely tear the kingdom from you ... Yet for the sake of David your father I will not do it in your days, but I will tear it out of the hand of your son' (1 Kings 11:5ff.).

See Fig. 16, p. 59

When Solomon died the northern region rejected his son Rehoboam as king, complaining of the 'hard service' and 'heavy yoke' (forced labour and taxes) Solomon had laid upon them. Contrary to his elders' advice Rehoboam boasted he would increase both. The kingdom split into two small, unstable, feuding nations – the kingdom of Israel with ten tribes in the north (later known as Samaria), and the kingdom of Judah with the tribes of Judah and Benjamin in the south. The capital of Judah was Jerusalem.

See Figs. 17a & 17b, pp. 60 & 61

Constant divisions within weakened both nations. They engaged in intermittent warfare with each other and neighbouring states, until the Assyrians conquered the kingdom of Israel in 721 BCE (2 Kings 17:6). 'The king of Assyria captured Samaria, and he carried the Israelites away to Assyria.' Most of the people of the ten tribes of Israel, still known as the 'Lost Tribes' today, were deported, dispersed and assimilated by other people, never to return. A relief commemorating the triumph and deportation was commissioned by the Assyrian King Sennacherib for his palace. The kingdom of Israel ceased to exist, and became an Assyrian province.

> And this was so, because the people of Israel had sinned against the Lord their God. ... They despised his statutes, and his covenant that he made with their fathers. ... They went after false idols, and became false, and they followed the nations that were around them. ... Therefore the Lord was very angry

ABRAHAM AND HIS DESCENDANTS

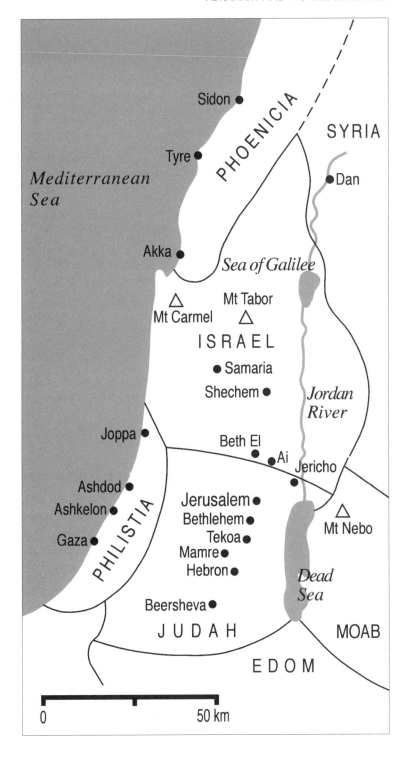

Figure 16: The division of Israel and Judah from 850 BCE. Israel and Philistia – annexed by the Assyrians, 722 BCE. Judah – overrun by the Babylonians, 586 BCE.

THE MYTHS THAT MAKE US

Figures 17a and 17b: Alabaster panels from King Sennacherib's palace, Ninevah, northern Iraq, c. 700–681 BCE, depicting the siege and capture of the city of Lachish in 701. Left: the Assyrian soldiers conquer the city. Right: soldiers carry away spoils of war; at the bottom right of the panel captive Israelites with what they can salvage being transported to other parts of the Assyrian Empire.
British Museum, London

with Israel, and removed them out of his sight; none was left but the tribe of Judah only. (2 Kings 17:7ff.)

They were severely punished by Yahweh, to the point of annihilation.

Marching south, the Assyrians captured some of Judah's territory and took thousands of survivors into exile: 'Judah also did not keep the commandments of the Lord their God, but walked in the customs which Israel introduced. And the Lord rejected all the descendants of Israel, and afflicted them, and gave them into the hand of the spoilers, until he cast them out of his sight.' (2 Kings 17:19, 20)

Jerusalem was spared on payment of a heavy indemnity, and the kingdom of Judah survived until 587 BCE when the Babylonians invaded.

All the leading priests and the people likewise were exceedingly unfaithful, following all the abominations of the nations. ... The wrath of the Lord rose against his people, till there was no remedy. ... Therefore he brought up against them the king of the Chaldeans [Nebuchadnezzar of Babylonia]. ... And they burned the house of God, and broke down the walls of

Jerusalem, and burned all its palaces with fire, and destroyed all its precious vessels. He took into exile in Babylon those who had escaped from the sword, and they became servants to him and his sons. (2 Chronicles 36:14ff.)

The deportation of Judahites to exile in Babylon became a theme of lament and remembrance for millennia to come –

By the waters of Babylon,
there we sat down and wept,
when we remembered Zion [Jerusalem] …

This psalm is a standard song today, but the original psalm has an unfortunate ending in the Yahwehist tradition –

Happy shall he be who takes your [Babylon's] little ones
and dashes them against the rock! (Psalm 137)

Despite the violent sentiments expressed in the psalm, the exiles were treated with tolerance in the diverse society that was Babylonia. They were free to maintain their own traditions and practise their

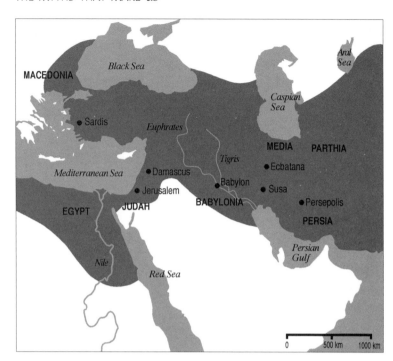

Figure 18: Map of the Persian Empire.

own religion. Many Jews learned a profitable way of life as merchants in Babylon, the great trading city. Although Hebrew remained the language of the Jewish religion and upper class, the exiles in Babylon learned to speak Aramaic, the *lingua franca* of Babylonian merchants and common language uniting the wide Babylonian area, and the language Jesus was later to speak. Two-thirds of the exiles chose to remain in the splendid cosmopolitan city when they were given freedom to return to Jerusalem by the Persian conqueror Cyrus the Great in 538 BCE. Yahweh was given credit for the humanity and compassion of Cyrus, a man from another culture and belief system – 'the Lord stirred up the spirit of Cyrus king of Persia' (2 Chronicles 36:22).

THE PERSIAN INFLUENCE: ZOROASTRIANISM

See Fig. 18, above

Cyrus the Great's empire stretched from the Aegean Sea (Macedonia) to the Indus River. He acquired this vast territory not only by warfare but also by diplomacy, with many territories submitting peacefully to him. He supported local customs, sacrificed to local deities and frequently appointed those he defeated to rule on his behalf. His leadership qualities were lauded by the Greeks and impressed

Figure 19: Persian agate cylinder seal, 5th century BCE. 'Darius, the great king', king of the Persian Empire, 521–486, is standing in his chariot hunting lions. The winged disc of Ahura Mazda is overhead.
British Museum, London

Alexander the Great and the Romans. It is no wonder that Cyrus (anointed by God in Isaiah 45:1–3) and his dynasty influenced Jewish thought. Legends of his beginnings are in the heroic tradition. His grandfather, the king Astyages, dreamed that Cyrus would grow up to overthrow him and ordered the child to be killed. Instead Cyrus was taken to a shepherd to be raised, and upon reaching manhood he revolted against his grandfather. Astyages' army deserted him and surrendered to Cyrus in 550 BCE.

The beliefs of Cyrus were based on the teachings of the religious reformer Zoroaster. Little is known about Zoroaster, but his beginnings also became legend.

> Zoroaster's mother was so filled with the Kingly Glory that she glowed in the dark. Zoroaster was conceived when the heavenly beings brought about the mingling of the Glory, spirit and body of the child in her womb. At his birth marvels and wonders took place one after another as a divine light flashed from his birthplace. Zoroaster's father, possessed by an evil demon, tried to kill his son several times. At the age of 30 Zoroaster was called to meet Ormazd (the Wise Lord), withstood three ordeals of fire, molten metal and knife, then

started his mission. He was killed by the foe of his religion.[9]

The similarity with the story in Matthew, the most Jewish of the Gospels, is striking. The writer of Matthew even has wise men from the East (Zoroastrian priests – Magi, from which our words 'magic' and 'magician' come) following the star (divine light) to Jesus' birthplace.

See Fig. 19, p.63

It is thought that Zoroaster refined already existing beliefs in the Wise Lord, Ahura Mazda (Ormazd) and his evil twin, the Lord of the Lie, Angra Mainyu (Ahiram). There was constant warfare between these forces of good and evil – good thoughts, words, and deeds against lies and deceit. (There is a psychological difference between a religion whose adherents believe the prime evil is disobedience, and one like Zoroastrianism which takes the prime evil to be lies and deceit.) According to Zoroaster, men and women are free to choose the path of righteousness or the path of wickedness and are responsible for their choices and subsequent actions. Righteousness has its reward in the afterlife, wickedness its retribution, with eventually a resurrection and judgement brought about by a returning Saviour, who will be born of a virgin. After three days, those judged as requiring and receiving punishment will be forgiven and will join Ormazd and dwell in total perfection.

> [Zoroaster was] the first to teach the doctrines of an individual judgement, Heaven and Hell, the future resurrection of the body, the general Last Judgement, and life everlasting for the united soul and body. These doctrines of faith were to become familiar articles of faith to much of mankind, through borrowings by Judaism, Christianity and Islam.[10]

Zoroastrian beliefs influenced the Pharisees, putting them in conflict with the traditional Temple Priests who adhered strictly to the Jewish-written Law of Moses. The Priests had great power since the Temple not only dictated religious policy but was also the Jewish treasury, bank and centre of authority. In contrast to the Temple Priests, the Pharisees were learned laymen. They believed in angels, longed for the future world of God, hoped for a promised Davidic Messiah who would destroy the power of the heathen, and believed in the resurrection of the dead with rewards and punishments in the world to come. Their beliefs were carried into Christianity by Paul, who was himself a Pharisee.

By the time of Jesus, the Persians had made Zoroastrianism the most powerful religion of the ancient world. It is no wonder that it affected later Judaism and Christianity – but with one big difference. Judaism could not accommodate or understand internal divinity, whereas Zoroastrianism held that man's foremost duty is to make his body the dwelling-place of the Bounteous Immortals. These are: Holy Spirit, Good Mind, Truth, Right-Mindedness, Kingdom, Wholeness and Immortality. It may be no coincidence that Jesus used the words 'Holy Spirit' ('Holy Ghost' in the King James Version) and 'Kingdom', Zoroastrian terms, not Old Testament terms. They are uniquely related to Jesus' teaching. ('Holy Spirit' is found only once in the Old Testament, Isaiah 6.)

Zoroastrianism continued in Persia until Muslim rule when many were persuaded or forced to embrace Islam. Between the 8th and 10th centuries CE most of the remaining Zoroastrians left Persia and settled in western India where they became known as Parsees, who are recognised today for their wealth, education and beneficence.

RETURN OF THE EXILES

The Jews who returned to Jerusalem from Babylon restored the Temple, spurning the assistance offered by the Samaritans, those members of the ten tribes of Israel who had escaped deportation by the Assyrians. They were termed 'adversaries of Judah and Benjamin' in Ezra 4, and this attitude continued at least to the time of Jesus.

The Jews had been exposed to a different culture and beliefs in Babylon. This led them to engage in speculations in late Judaism about heavenly Wisdom, a feminine figure that presents herself to humanity as mediator both in the work of creation and the knowledge of God. The first nine chapters of Proverbs, which date from after the exile in Babylon and may have been written by the Jews who remained there, introduce Wisdom as the most precious possession of humanity:

> Happy is the man who finds wisdom,
> and the man who gets understanding,
> for the gain from it is better than gain from silver
> and its profit better than gold.

> ...
> Long life is in her right hand;
> in her left hand are riches and honour.
> Her ways are ways of pleasantness,
> and all her paths are peace.
> She is a tree of life to those who lay hold of her;
> those who hold her fast are called happy.
> Get wisdom; get insight. (Proverbs 3:13ff.)

Here wisdom is combined with the tree of life as in other ancient myths. It appears to be the same wisdom Plato speaks of, a feminine principle of the soul that comes from knowing and understanding oneself. It also sounds like Jesus' kingdom of heaven – the buried treasure and pearl of very special value (Matthew 13:44ff.). The wise men who found the treasure and the pearl gave up everything to keep them. A priceless indwelling consciousness, the divinity within us all, waiting to be discovered.

For the first and only time in the Old Testament, the biblical creation myth is altered to include a female: 'Does not wisdom call, does not understanding raise her voice? ...'

> The Lord created me at the beginning of his work,
> the first of his acts of old.
> Ages ago I was set up,
> at the first, before the beginning of the earth.
> ... I was daily his delight,
> rejoicing before him always,
> rejoicing in his inhabited world
> and delighting in the sons of men. (Proverbs 8)

Here the Lord has a female consort and a balancing sacred marriage, and she was present at creation to become humanity's wisdom. Could Wisdom have been the serpent in the Garden of Eden after all? The Gospel of Luke – the most Greek of all the Gospels – has Jesus saying, 'Wisdom is justified by all her children' (Luke 7:35). However, she did not come into Western Christianity. If she had – if the concept of the One, a Whole with a female element, had been incorporated into the male Godhead – then our collective and individual history might well have been very different.

THE GREEK INFLUENCE

Two hundred years after the return from Babylon, Alexander the Great in his conquest of the Persian Empire conquered Judea (Judah) and the Jews became aware of Western philosophy for the first time. Alexander saw the area mainly as a corridor leading to Egypt and left the Jews undisturbed in their religion and customs, even allowing the High Priest to remain the head of the Jewish State. However, the Greeks had tremendous influence on the area, and a dialect of Greek was a *lingua franca* of the region well beyond the time of Jesus.

THE ROMANS

Rome had for some time been expanding its authority in the area, and in 63 BCE Pompey captured Jerusalem. Rome appointed Herod the Great, a Jewish Arab friendly to Rome, as king of Judea in 37 BCE and he ruled until 4 BCE, about the time of Jesus' birth. Herod's rule brought peace and prosperity to the area, marked by great building projects – massive fortresses, splendid cities (two being largely pagan), a magnificent palace, and a majestic temple. In his later years he became the centre of political and family intrigues.

After the death of Herod, the Romans shared his kingdom amongst his sons. Galilee was given to Herod Antipas, and the main part of Judea, Samaria and Idumaea (Edom) was eventually ruled by a series of Roman procurators. The fifth of these was Pontius Pilate.

Herod Antipas rebuilt at least two cities in Galilee modelled on Greek cities, and erected statues in the Greek manner in his palace. One of these cities, Sepphoris, was only five kilometres from Nazareth, and Herod Antipas made it his Galilean capital. He was a strong promoter of Greek culture and linked himself with well-to-do Jews who were tolerant of Roman authority.

Unrest was common and often bitter. The ruling Romans looked on Judea, Samaria and Galilee much as the Greeks had – a corridor between the far richer and more civilised lands of Syria and Egypt. They allowed Jews to practise their religion and exercise limited powers of administration and jurisdiction but they did not take kindly to insurrection or any show of terrorism, which they would suppress quickly and violently. The main troublemakers were a religio-political group called Zealots, probably founded by a Galilean – Galilee was known as a hotbed of insurrection. That Jesus was a Galilean and had at least one Zealot amongst his disciples – Simon – may well have added weight to his condemnation. The Zealots' goals were a Jewish nation based on Jewish Law, the rule of a prophesied king descended from the house of David who would restore the golden age, and the destruction of the hated, heathen Roman regime. Zealots carried out sudden raids on Roman forces and conducted a terrorist, guerrilla war from hiding places in the wilderness.* Eventually, some 35 years after Jesus' death, their actions culminated in the First Jewish Revolt which ended in the siege of Jerusalem and destruction of the Temple by the Romans in 70 CE. The Temple was never rebuilt, the Temple Priests were no more, and the Jewish religion became decentralised. Many Jews left for other parts of the Roman Empire. The Islamic Dome of the Rock and Al-Aqsa Mosque are now on the Temple Mount, which is believed to be the site of the ascension of the Prophet Mohammed through the seven heavens.

Not all Jewish citizens were antagonistic towards Rome. The wealthier elements of the society – the Temple Priests, aristocratic families and wealthy merchants – tended to have good relations with the Romans. The Priests' lives were so bound up with the Temple that when the Roman legions destroyed it they ceased to exist as a group. The Pharisees were not dominant in Jesus' time. They came to dominate after the disappearance of the Priests when the basis of the rabbinical Judaism of today was formed.

During the Roman occupation Greek culture and language continued to dominate. Some scholars believe that Jesus could speak the common Greek dialect, and possibly even read it. The current thought amongst some is that he was not the peasant of Christian tradition, but a woodworking artisan working on Herod Antipas' Greek buildings in Sepphoris. There he would have come into contact with all things Greek, including the philosophy.

Judaism had been brought in touch with four of the greatest civilisations of the ancient world – Babylonia, Persia, Greece and Rome. New ideas were presented to Jews and some of these ideas crept into their religion, some even more so into Christianity. The

---

* Terrorism is an action of underdogs who lack the force and weapons of those they see as foreign oppressors. In 1961 Nelson Mandela was head of Umkhonto we Sizwe ('Spear of the Nation'), an African National Congress armed force that carried out acts of sabotage as part of its campaign against apartheid.

Persians had the most profound effect, possibly because they were so admired as humanitarian liberators, they had a desert background with similar religious purity laws, and they came into contact with the Jews at a time when the Jews had been exposed to another, more tolerant, richer way of life in Babylon. The writer of Matthew obviously knew of Zoroastrian beliefs and wrote them into his story, just as Paul expressed his Pharisaic beliefs in his letters.

Despite all the contact it had with other beliefs Judaism did not let go of the external, all-powerful, male God of the Genesis creation myth. Jesus wished to change that. His whole ministry was about recognising the divinity within, but this is not what was taken to the west.

JESUS

As reported in all the Gospels, Jesus often became exasperated with his disciples' inability to understand his message.

> Do you not yet perceive or understand? Are your hearts hardened? Having eyes do you not see, and having ears do you not hear? And do you not remember? (Mark 8:17–18)
> [To Peter]: Get behind me, Satan! You are a hindrance to me; for you are not on the side of God, but of men. (Matthew 16:23)
> [To Philip]: Have I been with you so long, and yet you do not know me Philip? (John 14:9)

There is a story told in Luke 9:51ff.:

> [Jesus] set his face to go to Jerusalem. And he sent messengers ahead of him, who went and entered a village of the Samaritans, to make ready for him; but the people would not receive him, because his face was set towards Jerusalem. [Samaritans were antagonistic towards the Temple they had been excluded from, and all Temple worshippers.] And when his disciples James and John saw it, they said, 'Lord, do you want us to bid fire come down from heaven and consume them?' But he turned and rebuked them.

The disciples had no conception of what Jesus was teaching. Simple men brought up in the Jewish tradition, they found it impossible to step outside their ingrained beliefs – for example, that Samaritans were evil, of no account, and worthy of destruction. The disciples spread what they thought was the message of Jesus. But they did not grasp the respect for all humanity that Jesus taught and practised – respect that comes from appreciation of the divinity within all, which is a hallmark of mysticism.

THE MIRACLES

Much emphasis has been placed on the miracles of Jesus to prove his 'only-Son-of-God-ness'. However, travelling preachers and healers such as John the Baptist and Jesus were common at that time. Josephus, a Jewish priest, scholar and historian (37–100 CE), notes numerous instances of religious leaders who claimed to be prophets and obtained considerable followings. In her book, *A History of God*, Karen Armstrong writes, 'It has been pointed out that faith healers were familiar religious figures in Galilee: like Jesus they were mendicants, who preached, healed the sick and exorcised demons.'[1] Belief in possession by demons was common at the time. Donald Mackenzie confirms this in the ancient world in general, and tells of Babylonian beliefs and cures:

> Magicians baffled the demons by providing a charm … Or, perhaps the sacred water would dispel the evil one … When a pig was offered up in sacrifice as a substitute for a patient, the wicked spirit was commanded to depart and allow a kindly spirit to take its place.[2]

A story in Matthew, Mark and Luke tells of Jesus ordering the unclean spirits to come out and go into pigs who then rushed into the lake and were drowned (Matthew 8:28ff.; Mark 5:1; Luke 8:27).

Mackenzie describes the source of other cures:

> Saliva, like tears, had creative and therefore curative qualities; it also expelled and injured demons and brought good luck. Spitting ceremonies were referred to in the religious literature of Ancient Egypt. When the Eye of Ra [the Sun] was blinded by Set [a trickster sky god], Thoth [wise moon god] spat in it to restore vision.[3]

So the story of Jesus curing the blind man with his spit in Mark 8:22ff. and John 9:1ff. was based on a very ancient belief. The miraculous 'cures' attributed to Jesus in the Gospels were not new to the area, but his teachings were.

Miraculous accounts and legends were not only common in Near Eastern traditions, they can also be found in the Hellenistic, Greco-

Roman culture that influenced the development of early Christianity. Mark and Matthew mention Jesus complaining about the 'generation that asks for a sign' – the people wanting miracles. Cicero, the Roman scholar who lived from 106 to 43 BCE, commented that miracle stories may be necessary for the piety of ignorant folk, and Celsus, a 1st-century CE philosopher and medical writer, believed that Christian miracles, if they were genuine, did not offset such healings as those of the god Asclepius, the god of healing. Martin Luther dismissed 'outward miracles' disparagingly as 'jugglery' or 'apples and nuts for children'.[4] The miracle stories of Jesus may have been fabrications, as Cicero and Luther suggested, but it is the wisdom in Jesus' words that is important. Unfortunately, the miraculous acts attributed to him seem to have obscured this wisdom.

INFLUENCES

See Fig. 20, p. 73

Traditionally Jesus was thought to be a peasant who followed his father's trade of carpentry in the village of Nazareth in Galilee. With the archaeological discovery of the sophisticated Greek/Roman/Jewish city of Sepphoris (Zippori) only five kilometres west of Nazareth, however, ideas about Jesus have changed. Situated on important inland roads linking north and south, east and west, Sepphoris was a thriving commercial community, with many traders and travellers coming and going. Satellite villages around the city supplied it with food and labour, and Nazareth was such a village. Herod Antipas rebuilt Sepphoris along Greek lines after it had been destroyed by the Romans about 6 BCE during a Galilean riot. Herod made the city his showplace Galilean capital. It is likely that Jesus and his father were employed during this rebuilding, possibly not as carpenters but as artisans. To work there Jesus would have had to understand the Greek dialect used as the common language in the Roman Empire. He could well have come into contact with all the diversities of thought found in that Empire, and particularly with Greek philosophy.

As ideas travelled along caravan routes in the past, in Jesus' time they travelled more rapidly along well-built Roman roads. Only 500 kilometres from Sepphoris was the Egyptian city of Alexandria – a centre of Jewish learning and Greek scholarship and science. At the time of Jesus the city had the largest population of Jews outside

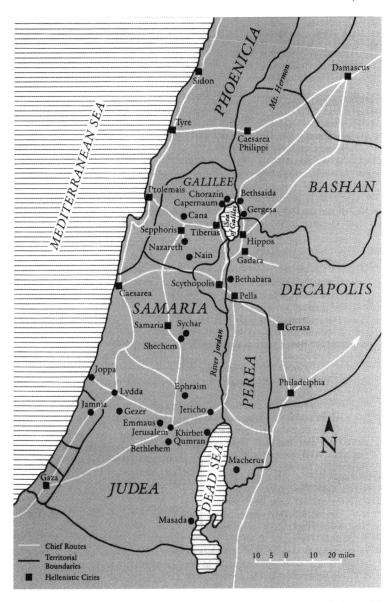

Figure 20: Palestine in the 1st century CE.

Palestine. According to tradition the first translation of the Old Testament from Hebrew to Greek (the Septuagint translation) was produced there in the 3rd and 2nd centuries BCE. Another tradition has St Mark, the supposed Gospel writer, preaching in Alexandria in the mid-1st century CE.

The Platonist philosopher Philo Judaeus was born 10 to 25 years before Jesus. As a devout Jew, Philo made at least one pilgrimage from his home in Alexandria to Jerusalem. He attempted to reconcile the Jewish God of his faith with the Greek God of his learning and experience. This was difficult because, as Karen Armstrong points out, 'a chasm separated Yahweh from the world but Greeks believed that the gift of reason made human beings kin to God; they could, therefore, reach him by their own efforts.'[5] Philo used the Greek word *enthousiasmos*, 'having God within one', in his writings. He believed that God has implanted a mystical love of God in man, through which man becomes Godlike. Like Plato, he believed that divinity resides within the soul and humans can reach that divinity – in fact, they yearn for that direct experience.

Philo may not have gone to Sepphoris and Jesus may not have gone to Alexandria, but Greek knowledge/thinking was known in the area at that time. As Philo was a Jew his ideas may have been widely discussed – possibly even scoffed at – in the learned Jewish world, and Plato's ideas were well known in the wide-flung Greek world of Roman occupation. We know nothing of Jesus until he started his ministry at about the age of 30. He could well have been exposed to Greek philosophy, possibly even Philo's philosophy, found it meant something to him, and then attempted to teach it. If one intelligent Jewish mind, Philo's, could assimilate ideas of the soul as the divinity within, so could another – that of Jesus. It is not difficult to surmise that both Philo and Jesus had mystical experiences. From what Jesus taught we may also surmise that he knew about inner divinity from first-hand experience. He called it 'the Kingdom of God' and 'Kingdom of Heaven'. The concept was beyond the comprehension of his followers, who were steeped in Jewish tradition.

When Jesus died his followers decided he was the awaited Messiah from the house of David. Paul preached that Jesus was the only son of God, the anointed Saviour, and his death and resurrection was the mechanism for the salvation of humankind through the sacrificial death of Jesus, later known as atonement. These beliefs are the foundation of Western Christianity.

Paul expected the end of the world, the Last Judgement and the new world of God to happen in his lifetime. Paul got it wrong. He wanted Jesus to be the fulfiller of Jewish prophecy and presented him that way. He did not meet Jesus or ever hear him speak, and had little contact with the so-called Jesus Movement* led by Jesus' brother, James, and the apostles Peter and John in Jerusalem. Paul met James

---

* A more accurate term than 'early Christianity' since at this time it was a movement still within Judaism.

and Peter very briefly before he started on his self-appointed ministry. It would appear that Paul and the Jerusalem sect did not agree on many points and there were arguments. Many in the Jerusalem sect wanted the Jesus Movement to stay within Judaism, for example to observe circumcision and other prescriptions of the Mosaic Law such as not eating with Gentiles. Paul disagreed with this. The Jerusalem sect eventually denied the legitimacy of Paul's apostolic calling.

At the centre of Jesus' teaching was the Kingdom of God, but central to Paul's teaching was the Christ sacrificed and risen. Paul went west and preached to the Gentiles and the Jews living in the Diaspora – and there were many. His letters are the first 'Christian' writings we have, predating the writing of the Gospels. The first letter was 1 Thessalonians, dating from about 50 CE, twenty years after Jesus' crucifixion, and ten years before the first Gospel was written.

THE GOSPELS

In the Gospels Jesus frequently spoke of the Kingdom of God and its imminence but he obviously did not mean the end of the world, as Paul proclaimed. The first Gospel written, Mark's (c. 60 CE), has Jesus' opening proclamation: 'The kingdom of God is at hand; repent, and believe in the gospel.' The words 'repent' or 'convert' are both more harsh than the original Greek word *metanoeite*, which literally means 'change your minds'. As Thomas Cahill points out,

> The word certainly refers to a spiritual turnaround, but the change that is looked for here is an openness to something new and unheard of. … Our word 'gos'pel', an Anglo-Saxon elision of 'good spell' (meaning 'good word' or 'good news'), is the Old English translation of the Greek *euaggelion*, meaning *the* good news.[6]

Mark's Gospel is considered the most reliable. It does not mention the divine conception, and the original manuscript finished at chapter 16:8, with those who found the empty tomb being terrified: 'And they went out and fled from the tomb; for trembling and astonishment had come upon them; and they said nothing to any one, for they were afraid.' There is no mention of Jesus rising from the dead, his appearing to the disciples, or his being taken up into heaven. It is presumed that verses 9–20 were added later by another writer.

The Gospels of Matthew and Luke were written about fifteen years later, after the destruction of the Jerusalem Temple in 70 CE, which saw the end of the Temple priests and sacrifice, and the rise of the Pharisees. Until then the 'Jesus Movement' had been part of Judaism in Jerusalem. With decentralisation from the priests and the Temple to the Pharisees and the synagogues, an irrevocable split widened as those of the new movement put more and more emphasis on Jesus rather than the Law of Moses. This caused friction between members of the movement and the Pharisees, as reported in Matthew. The writer of Matthew wrote with unbridled antagonism about his own time. At the time of Jesus the Pharisees' argument was with the Temple priests, not with Jesus.

The Gospels of Matthew and Luke have much of the content, sometimes word-for-word, of the Gospel of Mark – Matthew more than 90 per cent and Luke more than 50 per cent. The Gospel according to John was written about seventy years after Jesus' death, 100 CE, and did not use Mark as a source. At this time the letters of Paul had been gathered together for general circulation. They quickly became a standard reference for 'Christian' teaching.

THE GOSPEL OF THOMAS

In 1945 the Gospel of Thomas, a possible source for all four biblical Gospels, was unearthed near the town of Nag Hammadi in Upper Egypt (see Appendix 1). Fragments of the gospel had been found in the 1890s, but the the first complete Thomas gospel was found at Nag Hammadi. In the introduction to a translation of the document, Helmut Koester writes: 'A large number of the sayings of the *Gospel of Thomas* have parallels in the gospels of the New Testament, in the Synoptic Gospels [Matthew, Mark, and Luke], as well as the Gospel of John.' As Thomas contains only the sayings of Jesus without any story, Professor Koester states that it is unlikely that Thomas borrowed from the New Testament Gospels. When considering the form and wording, he writes, 'The *Gospel of Thomas* almost always appears to have preserved a more original form of the traditional sayings.'[7] Elaine Pagels supports this idea, and mentions that Professor Koester 'has suggested that the collection of sayings in the *Gospel of Thomas* … may include some traditions even *older* than the gospels of the

New Testament, ... as early as, or earlier, than Mark, Matthew, Luke and John.'[8] The Jesus Seminar, a group of scholars from a wide array of Western religious traditions and academic institutions, place the writing of Thomas at the same time as those of Paul, 50–60 CE.

See Fig. 21, below

The gospel opens with the words: 'Here are the secret sayings which Jesus the Living spoke, and which Didymus Jude Thomas wrote down.' We are told in the New Testament that Jesus would withdraw and explain to his disciples what he had said in public. The Thomas gospel appears to be verbatim records of these private sessions, with little or no editing. It is suspected the New Testament Gospels were edited over the years before they became standardised; we know Mark had 12 verses added to the end and it appears the last chapter of John was added later.

Many of the sayings and stories told by Jesus in *Thomas* are also in the New Testament – for example, the scattered seeds falling on different ground; giving to Caesar what belongs to Caesar; the merchant finding the pearl. But there are sayings in *Thomas* that are not in the Bible. An example is saying 3:

> Jesus said: 'If those who lead You say to You: "See, the Kingdom is in heaven!" then the birds of the sky will be there before You. If they say to You, "It is in the sea!" then the fish will be there before You. But the Kingdom is inside You and outside You. When You know yourselves, then You will be known, and You will know that You are the children of the Living Father. But if You do not know yourselves, then You dwell in poverty; then You are that poverty.'

Figure 21: Gospel writing timetable.

40 CE	
50 CE	Thomas Paul
60 CE	Mark
70 CE	
	Matthew, Luke
80 CE	
90 CE	
100 CE	
	John
110 CE	

The message is clear: the kingdom is within, found by knowing and understanding oneself. Jesus had to be very careful what he said about his beliefs, and who he said them to, as blasphemy was punishable by stoning to death under Mosaic Law. Stephen, who is known as the first Christian martyr, was stoned to death for blasphemy (Acts 6–8). Reading *Thomas*, we realise what an ever-present problem this must have been for Jesus, and why he used obscure language such as 'the kingdom'. He expressed himself fully only to those he trusted:

> (13) ... And He took [Thomas] aside and spoke three words to him. When Thomas came back to his companions, they asked him: 'What did Jesus say to You?' Thomas answered

them: 'If I tell You one of the words he said to me, You will take up stones and throw them at me ...'

Yet what Jesus taught did reach into some areas of early Christianity. A statement attributed to Monoimus, a later teacher, could well be taken to express Jesus' beliefs:

> Abandon the search for God and the creation and other matters of similar sort. Look for him by taking yourself as the starting point. Learn who it is within you who makes everything his own and says, 'My God, my mind, my thought, my soul, my body.' Learn the sources of sorrow, joy, hate ... If you carefully investigate these matters you will find him in yourself.[9]

Monoimus was a Gnostic – an adherent of Gnosticism, a way of thought declared heretical at the end of the 2nd century CE by nascent Christendom. The Greek word *gnosis* means knowledge. But as the Gnostics use the term, it is more accurately translated 'insight', for *gnosis* involves an intuitive process of knowing oneself. And to know oneself, the Gnostics claimed, is to know human nature and human destiny.

Despite the threat of heresy in the Western Church, mystics too have expressed beliefs very similar to those of Jesus. Meister Eckhart (1250–1329), a German Dominican priest, was a 'mystic and prophet, feminist and philosopher, preacher and theologian, administrator and poet, a spiritual genius and declared heretic'.[10] One of the charges against him was that he claimed that God himself was born in the soul. He said, for example,

> The seed of God is in us.
> Now the seed of a pear tree
>   grows into a pear tree;
> and a hazel seed
>   grows into a hazel tree;
> a seed of God
>   grows into God.[11]

Many of Jesus' metaphors are explained in this simple passage.

The seed of God is in the soul:

> God is nowhere so truly as in the soul ... in the inmost soul, in the summit of the soul.[12]

And the soul is female:

> Whatever the soul effects, she effects with her powers. What she understands, she understands with the intellect. What she remembers, she does with the memory ...[13]

Once the inner kingdom is recognised there is no need for further instruction:

> that in whatever soul God's kingdom dawns, which knows God's kingdom is near her, is in no need of sermons and teaching: she is instructed by it and is assured of eternal life...[14]

Paul did not understand 'the kingdom' in this way, and neither has Christianity. Over the centuries 'the kingdom' has been interpreted in many different ways. Paul understood it apocalyptically, as have various Christian sects (for example, the Jehovah's Witnesses). Augustine, in the 5th century, understood the Church to be the historical representative of the Kingdom of God on Earth. Other Christians have taken the kingdom to be God's active rule in the world requiring obedience, or to be available only to the faithful after death. None of these doctrines can be attributed to Jesus. In Luke, Jesus states to the Pharisees: 'The kingdom of God is not coming with signs to be observed; nor will they say, "Lo, here it is!" or "There!" for behold, the kingdom of God is in the midst of you' (Luke 17:21). This is very similar to saying 113 in *Thomas*:

> His disciples said to Him: 'When will the Kingdom come?' Jesus said: 'It does not come by expecting it. It will not be a matter of saying: "See, it is here!" or: "Look, it is there!" Rather, the Kingdom of the Father is spread over the earth and men do not see it.'

LOVE

The second message of Jesus concerns love – 'Love your enemies'. He showed respect and understanding for traditional enemies such as the Samaritans, the ruling Romans (hated in some quarters), those considered beyond the pale (such as tax collectors and prostitutes) or impure (the physically and mentally ill and disabled), males and females alike. Respect and understanding is the 'love' Jesus commended – a recognition that all humanity is the same, with the same inner divinity. This was a Greek idea, the 'oneness' of humanity. It was not part of Judaism with its strict religious, purity and marriage laws that set them apart. The Greeks envisaged the civilised world as a multiracial, multinational society.

The 'oneness' of the Greeks was conveyed by the Platonist notion that 'the immortal mind in me is just the same as the immortal mind in you. That mind, in fact, is God.'

> We carry the image of truth in us, and we do so not from chance and natural selection, but from our origin, which is also the world's origin. ... We are the offspring of the selfsame intellect that engenders the ordered universe. ... 'The Good' and 'the One' are different names for It, for something that makes it possible for anything to be thought, which cannot itself be the object of rational thought.[15]

There is a common pattern in all these teachings. Know yourself and you will find the divinity within (God, the Good, the One, the Kingdom, the immortal mind, the soul). Once this divinity is recognised it will be seen that all other humans have the same divinity, indeed all creation has it – 'the Kingdom is inside You, and outside You.' From the knowledge of inner divinity comes Oneness, the love that Jesus spoke of, respect and understanding. In the words of the American writer James Baldwin, 'To encounter oneself is to encounter the other – and this is love.' And in the Thomas gospel we read:

> (22) ... Jesus said to them: 'When You make the two one, and when You make the inside like the outside and the outside like the inside, and the above like the below, and when You make the male and the female one, so that the male will not be male

nor the female female ... then will You enter the Kingdom.'

(61) ... Jesus said to [Salome]: 'Therefore I say, if somebody is one, he will be full of light, but if he is divided, he will be full of darkness.'

Similar thoughts have been expressed over the centuries:

All are but parts of one stupendous whole,
Whose body is nature, and God the soul.
Alexander Pope

The true nature of religion is ... the immediate consciousness of the Deity as He is found in ourselves and in the world.
Friedrich Schleiermacher

When you see that God is the creation, and that you are the creature, you realise that God is within you, and in the man or woman with whom you are talking as well.
Joseph Campbell

We were born to make manifest the glory of God that is within us; it's in Everyone!
Nelson Mandela

None of this is central to Christian belief.

DEATH

On the subject of death, we find the following in the Thomas gospel:

(1) And He said: 'He who penetrates the meaning of these words will not taste death.'
(18) The disciples said to Jesus: 'Tell us how our end will be.' Jesus said: 'So have You discovered the beginning, that You look for the end? For where the beginning is, there the end will be. Fortunate is he who stands at the beginning; he will know the end and will not taste death.'

This removes the fear of death: we were divine before we were born, and we die to return to that divine form. We live in a cyclical pattern rather than linear time with a beginning and end.

Paul interpreted death in a very different way, as a punishment – a punishment going back to the creation myth: 'Sin came into the world through one man and death through sin, and so death spread to all men because all men sinned … For as by one man's disobedience many were made sinners, so by one man's obedience many will be made righteous' (Romans 5:12ff.). So, through Paul's teaching, Christianity came to be based on the sin of humanity requiring a saviour for redemption.

CHRISTIANITY

Nothing is more difficult than competing with a myth.
– Françoise Giroud

'Had there been no Fall, there would be no need for Redemption. The image of the Fall is, therefore, essential to the [Western] Christian myth.'[1] According to this myth, the sin of Adam was atoned for by the sacrifice of Jesus. In the Letter of Paul to the Ephesians, probably written by one of Paul's disciples, we read that Jesus 'gave himself up on your behalf as an offering and sacrifice'. Sacrifice, prevalent in all primitive religions, was a central theme in Judaism until the destruction of the Temple and disappearance of the Priests in 70 CE. The end of ritual sacrifice effectively marks the demise of ancient Judaism. Prayer and study became central to Judaism, whereas Paul's writings carried the idea of the sacrificial death of Jesus into Christianity.

SACRIFICE

A 'sin offering' was an important Jewish ritual described in the Old Testament book Leviticus. To purify guilt and re-establish the holy bond with God, an unblemished animal was sacrificed and the blood of the consecrated animal was sprinkled on the altar and elsewhere. Paul was steeped in the Judaism of his day and saw the life of Jesus, culminating in death, as the supreme sacrifice. The shedding of Jesus' blood wiped out the sin of humankind, and a new relationship of eternal life was established between God and humans.

One of the things Jesus wanted to eradicate was ritual sacrifice: 'Go and learn what this means, "I desire mercy, and not sacrifice."' (Matthew 9:13). His act of 'cleansing the Temple' bears this out. It happened at Passover, the celebration of the release of the Hebrews from Egypt. According to Exodus 12:21, the blood of a sacrificed sheep was used to mark Hebrew homes to be spared from God's last plague, which killed all the Egyptian first-born. A mark of blood on the doorpost was the sign for God to 'pass over' that household. During this sacred festival the Temple became a giant abattoir with the ritual slaughter of thousands of animals and birds. The Temple was a strange mixture of splendour and squalor: the glittering exterior of gold and shining white stone, 'the elaborate and beautiful ritual, the vestments, the jewels, the incense and chants contrasting strangely with [the bellowing cattle], the blood, guts, flies and stench that must have hung continually over the great altar, despite the elaborate arrangements made for drainage and ablution'.[2] When Jesus entered this place and saw creatures for sale to be slaughtered, with moneychangers changing currencies to the 'holy shekels' that were needed to pay Temple taxes, his anger knew no bounds:

> He entered the temple and began to drive out those who sold and those who bought in the temple, and he overturned the tables of the moneychangers and the seats of those who sold pigeons; and he would not allow any one to carry anything through the temple. And he taught, and said to them, 'Is it not written, "My house shall be called a house of prayer for all the nations"?* But you have made it a den of robbers.' (Mark 11:15ff.; also Matthew 21:12ff.; Luke 19:45ff.; John 2:14ff.)

This is one of the few events that appear in all four gospels. Mark, Matthew and Luke place it at the end of Jesus' ministry, John at the beginning. Jesus was demonstrating against the administration of the Temple Priests, and his abhorrence of sacrifice – he would not allow any animals to pass through that court to be slaughtered. He stopped the killing, but for only a short time. How ironic that he came to represent what he abhorred. Paul presented him as the ultimate sacrifice for the ultimate sin.

But Jesus was speaking for many of his time:

> In the minds of many devout Jews, especially of the Dispersion, a more spiritual conception of the Deity than a god who delighted in the flesh of bulls and sheep was developing; already the synagogue, where instruction was given, the Law read, and prayer offered, had become the religious centre for thousands. Already in Jerusalem there were numbers of synagogues.[3]

---

* Isaiah 56:7 - 'For my house shall be called a house of prayer for all peoples.'

And Jesus was expressing views that had been around for up to 700 years. See, for example, Isaiah 1:11 and 16:

> What to me is the multitude of your sacrifices? says the Lord;
> I have enough of your burnt offerings of rams and the fat of fed beasts;
> I do not delight in the blood of bulls,
> or of lambs, or of he goats.
> ...
> Wash yourselves, make yourselves clean;
> remove the evil of your doings from before my eyes;
> cease to do evil,
> learn to do good;
> seek justice,
> correct oppression;
> defend the fatherless,
> plead for the widow.

It was all to happen 40 years after Jesus died, when the Temple was destroyed and the Priests were no more. Modern Judaism is very different from the Judaism of Jesus' day.

SIN

The great sin that needed atonement was the sin of disobedience committed by Adam: 'You may freely eat of every tree of the garden; but of the tree of the knowledge of good and evil you shall not eat, for in the day that you eat of it you shall die' (Genesis 2:16). Adam ate from that tree and was punished by banishment from God's presence, along with toil, suffering and no access to the Tree of Life. Disobedience became the worst sin humans could commit.

The New Testament is translated from Greek. The Greek word translated by 'sin' – *hamartanein* – is an archery term, meaning 'miss the mark'. If you miss the mark then you must correct your aim. This is very different from the Christian idea of sin, as the 19th-century theologian Theodore Parker explains,

> They (sc. the heathen of classical antiquity) were conscious of

wrath, of cruelty, avarice, drunkenness, lust, sloth, cowardice, and other actual vices, and struggled and got rid of the deformities, but they were not conscious of 'enmity against God' and didn't sit down and whine and groan against non-existent evil. I have done wrong things enough in my life, and do them now: I miss the mark, draw bow, and try again.[4]

In other religions there was no striving for unattainable 'perfection'. The ancient deities were not perfect: for example they neglected their crops in the Sumerian creation myth, and upset their great-grandparents in the Babylonian creation myth. In ancient Greek thought, sin was looked upon as a failure on the part of a person to reach their potential, to achieve their true self expression and to preserve their due relation to the rest of the universe. This was attributed mainly to ignorance. The Greek philosopher Socrates held that no one does wrong willingly: to act is always to do what one thinks is good, or thinks will have a better effect than any known alternative. If one does something wrong, it must be through ignorance, and so 'wrongdoers' need only be taught their error. (Socrates himself said that he had an inner divine voice – a *daemon* – that would warn him when he was about to take a wrong step.) Teaching wrongdoers their error – giving them 'known alternatives' (choices) – is very difficult in our culture, as the dominant interpretation of our creation myth is that all humans are sinners, for whom punishment, not teaching alternative behaviour, is required.

Jesus did not mention the sin of Adam in the New Testament, and it was not part of his philosophy. The concept came from Paul – 'One man's trespass led to condemnation for all men' (Romans 5:18) – and was later developed into Original Sin by the Church Fathers. Augustine, Bishop of Hippo in Roman Africa from 396 to 430, set the stage for the times that followed when he wrote:

> Banished [from Paradise] after his sin, Adam bound his offspring also with the penalty of death and damnation, that offspring which by sinning he had corrupted in himself, as in a root; so that whatever progeny was born (through carnal concupiscence, by which a fitting retribution for his disobedience was bestowed upon him) from himself and his spouse – who was the cause of his sin and the companion of his damnation – would drag through the ages the burden of

Original Sin, by which it would itself be dragged through manifold errors and sorrows, down to that final and never ending torment with the rebel angels ... so the matter stood; it was falling headlong from one wickedness to another; and joined in the faction of the angels who had sinned, it was paying the most righteous penalty of impious treason.[5]

And so it came to be Christian dogma that human nature had been so corrupted by Adam's fall that the human will, though free, was able to will only what was sinful until blessed with divine grace. Although Augustine may have meant that divine grace was available by direct contact with God, it came to be believed that it was available only through the Christian church.

Over a thousand years later Augustine's thoughts were reinforced by the founders of Protestantism. In 1559, John Calvin, whose influence has persisted in most Protestant churches, wrote: 'Original sin is seen to be an hereditary depravity and corruption of nature, diffused into all parts of the soul ... For our nature is not merely bereft of good but is so productive of every kind of evil that it cannot be inactive.'[6]

Thus our creation myth, as interpreted by the founders of Christianity, gave rise to the belief that our core, our very souls were evil – 'And there is no health in us.' It became necessary to plead with God to 'Have mercy upon us miserable sinners.' Divine grace was available only to members of a Christian church.

In sum, the doctrine of salvation, basic to Christianity, is that man is deserving of damnation by God for Original Sin, which he inherits by descent from Adam, and for his own actual sin. Jesus' crucifixion is seen as a vicarious sacrifice offered to God as propitiation or atonement for human sin. Or, because sin is thought to put man in the power of the devil, it may be seen as the price paid to redeem man from the devil. In any case, belief in the saving power of Jesus is fundamental to Christianity.

But here is one of the main weaknesses of Christianity in this modern age. For many, the underlying creation myth is no longer believable, and so there is no need of a saviour.

However, belief in this creation myth has given tremendous licence over the ages to mistreat those of other faiths – the justification being that they are sinners who have not been saved by Jesus' sacrifice, because they either do not know about it or have rejected the idea.

The justification survives today. Original Sin 'is a veritable weapon in the hands of those bent on controlling others'.⁷ But this does not sit well with the respect and understanding Jesus practised and preached.

WOMEN

The group in Western society that has suffered most from the formalisation of Christianity is women. Once again the justification comes from the creation myth. Eve, 'the mother of all who live', was demonised, and so by gender alone were all women. Tertullian, an important early Christian theologian, wrote:

> Do you not know that you are each an Eve? The sentence of God on this sex of yours lives in this age: the guilt must of necessity live too. *You* are the devil's gateway; *you* are the unsealer of that forbidden tree; *you* are the first deserter of the divine law; *you* are she who persuaded him whom the devil was not valiant enough to attack. *You* so carelessly destroyed man, God's image. On account of *your* desert, even the Son of God had to die.⁸

If Tertullian had said that under Hammurabian Law in Babylonia 1500 years earlier, he would have been branded on the forehead.

And so women have been relegated to a lower order over the ages. In most Christian countries women were not given equal voting rights with men until the 20th century.* In the United States and Great Britain the vote was granted to women only after bitter struggles. Two crucially important professions with a high proportion of women – nursing and primary school teaching – have been neglected and underpaid over the years. Today equal pay for equal work by women is still an issue in some quarters, and motherhood is often not given the respect and understanding it deserves. Once again this does not sit well with what Jesus actually taught. Elaine Pagels writes in her

---

* New Zealand (1893), Australia (1902), Finland (1906), Norway (1913). Between 1914 and 1939 women in 28 countries were granted equal voting rights with men, they included Soviet Russia (1917), Canada (1918), Germany, Austria, Poland, and Czechoslovakia (1919), the United States and Hungary (1920), and Great Britain (1928).

book *The Gnostic Gospels*:

> Jesus himself violated Jewish convention by talking openly with women, and he included them among his companions … Some ten to twenty years after Jesus' death, certain women held positions of leadership in local Christian groups; women acted as prophets, teachers, and evangelists. … By the end of the second century, women's participation in worship was explicitly condemned: groups in which women continued on to leadership were branded as heretical.[9]

Some of Paul's first converts were women and he honoured them for this. However, Paul was steeped in Jewish tradition, as shown by such passages as this:

As in all the churches of the saints, the women should keep silence in the churches. For they are not permitted to speak, but should be subordinate, as even the law says. If there is anything they desire to know, let them ask their husbands at home. For it is shameful for a woman to speak in church. (1 Corinthians 14:33ff.)

So we have in Christian churches the exclusive male priesthood and ministry, only recently rectified, and then only in some denominations. As the power of the Christian creation myth declines, the freedom and status of women increases.

Paul taught that women were created as lesser beings than men:

[Man] is the image and glory of God; but woman is the glory of man (For man was not made from woman, but woman from man. Neither was man created for woman, but woman for man.). (1 Corinthians 11:7ff.)

Women in Western history have been subjected to the men in their lives. For example, the marriage service in the Anglican Book of Common Prayer has the bride promising to obey her husband. English common law removed the separate legal personality of a woman when she married and merged it in that of her husband, so that the husband acquired extensive rights to the administration and ownership of her property, including full ownership of any money she received from employment or business. This is very different from ancient Sumer and Babylonia. Under the Code of Hammurabi, 18th century BCE, a married woman possessed her own property, and the power vested in her father was never transferred to her husband. Under Roman law, wives sometimes had a position of independence in regard to their property, and Muslim women have traditionally owned and managed their own property and been included in inheritance. The emancipation of women dating from the latter part of the 19th century in the West has had a profound effect on family law and the law regarding marital property. It has taken a long time for our Christian society to catch up with some ancient societies.

THE SACRED

A drastic consequence of Paul's concentration on the Genesis creation myth was to spread the Judaic idea of removing divinity, not only from humanity, but from all creation. As Joseph Campbell puts it:

> In the bible, God and man, from the beginning, are distinct. Man is made in the image of God, indeed, and the breath of God has been breathed into his nostrils; yet his being, his self, is not that of God, nor is it one with the universe. The fashioning of the world, of the animals, and of Adam (who then became Adam and Eve) was accomplished not within the sphere of divinity but outside of it.[10]

Mother Earth and Mother Nature were no longer divine. Awe at the mysteries of humanity and the world were done away with. The miracles of conception, gestation and birth of all living creatures, the marvel of seeds having innate memories of what to become, the wonders and movements of the universe, the beauty of a fiery sunset, sacred groves, sacred trees and sacred animals were all eradicated from Western thinking. It is possible that we lost our respect for Earth and Nature because of this radical sundering of divinity and nature. Sacredness in Christianity went into a Sacred Book, a Sacred History, Sacred Churches, Sacred Rituals (all man-made) and a Sacred Sacrifice by a Sacred Man – only one Sacred Being divinely conceived who was crucified, dead, buried and rose again.

'VIRGIN BIRTH'

The first mention of Jesus' birth appears in Paul's letter to the Galatians. He had earlier established Jesus' divinity by his resurrection in his Letter to the Romans, 1:2ff. Paul writes in Galatians 4:4 that Jesus was 'born of woman' with no mention of divine conception or 'virgin birth'.

Some years later the writers of both Matthew and Luke appear to refer to a virgin conception, the child Jesus being conceived by the Holy Spirit. Matthew, the most Jewish of the Gospel writers, knew his Jewish prophecies well. Matthew 1:23 quotes the prophecy from Isaiah 7:14, which says, according to the King James Version and the New International Version: 'Behold, a virgin shall conceive and bear a son, and shall call his name Immanuel.' But in the Revised Standard Version the prophecy is translated using the words 'young woman' instead of 'virgin'. In *Near Eastern Mythology*, John Gray writes: '"Virgin" is a mistranslation of the Hebrew "*almah*", which means in fact "a young woman sexually mature", bearing or capable of bearing her first child, which signifies the early teens in the East.'[11]

Luke was the most Greek of the Gospel writers. Many Greek myths have virgins conceiving by the great god Zeus and giving birth to sons, for example, Dionysos (Bacchus) and Herakles (Hercules). The Greeks accepted an exceptional man or god-man as being the son of the supreme god and a virgin.

The first and last Gospels written, Mark and John, do not mention divine conception. However, myths surround the conception of at least three other great religious leaders – the Buddha, Zoroaster, and Lao Tzu. The Buddha's mother had a dream that a beautiful elephant, a creature from heaven, white as silver, entered her womb through her side. Lao Tzu, the traditional originator of Taoism, was conceived by a shooting star.

The Gospels of Matthew and Luke both have Bethlehem as the birthplace of Jesus. It is now believed more likely that Jesus was born in his home village of Nazareth. However, a prophecy in Micah 5:2 states 'But you, O Bethlehem Ephrathah [Judah], who are little to be among the clans of Judah, from you shall come forth for me one who is to be ruler of Israel, whose origin is from of old, from ancient days.' Matthew 2:6 makes his story fit this prophecy. Bethlehem was the presumed birthplace and home of David, and the prophesied

Messiah was to be descended from the house of David. According to Luke, however, the reason for Joseph and Mary to go to Bethlehem, 'the city of David', was an enrolment or census because Joseph was 'of the house and lineage of David' (Luke 2:4).

CRUCIFIXION

The Romans used crucifixion to get rid of political agitators and to warn other agitators of the horror that could be their fate. The Roman authorities were especially alert at the time of the Passover in Jerusalem as thousands of pilgrims flooded into the city, making the population swell from 50,000 to 150,000. Political/religious dissidents could cause upheaval and riots with their acts of terrorism, threatening the peace. Surveillance and crowd control were at a premium. If Jesus 'cleansed the temple' as reported in all four New Testament Gospels he would have been viewed as a threat to the Pax Romana, particularly with the crowds following him. His disruptive act would have brought him to the attention of the Roman garrison that overlooked the Temple. Having been labelled a trouble-maker, a dissident likely to upset the peace of Rome, his fate was sealed. There is no doubt that he was crucified by the Romans for sedition, and the Temple priests who were comfortable with the status quo feared him for a similar reason.

Crucifixion entails a long, slow, painful death. It usually took two days or more for exhaustion or heart failure to finish a life. Death could be hastened by shattering the legs so that shock and asphyxiation set in. Jesus did not have his legs shattered, and yet Mark reports he died, amazingly, in six hours or less. Pilate was surprised that he had died so quickly, and he would know because he had had many crucified. John gives a very interesting description:

> Since it was the day of Preparation, in order to prevent the bodies from remaining on the cross on sabbath, (for that sabbath was a high day), the Jews asked Pilate that their legs might be broken, and that they might be taken away. So the soldiers came and broke the legs of the first, and of the other who had been crucified with him; but when they came to Jesus and saw that he was already dead, they did not break his legs. (John 19:31ff.)

Jesus was a man used to sustained prayer and meditation, which gave him the ability to slow his breathing and heart rate. To escape physical pain during the crucifixion he would have been capable of putting himself into a deep deathlike trance. Moreover, there may have been an opiate, or a mixture made from the mandrake plant with narcotic properties in the sour wine he drank just before he collapsed (mentioned in Mark, Matthew and John). When he was taken down from the cross he was wrapped with the antiseptic soothing herbs of myrrh and aloes (note: healing herbs rather than embalming ones). He was left in a new tomb, undisturbed because of the sabbath, for 36 hours. From there he was taken dead or alive by human hands. Mark's original manuscript ends at this point, with the discovery of an empty tomb. Jesus may have died and his body may have been taken from the tomb. This idea is not new. The German philosopher and scholar Hermann Reimarus (1694–1768) concluded, after trying to reconcile the four different accounts of the resurrection told in the Gospels, that 'the disciples, distraught by the unexpected end to the ministry of Jesus, stole his crucified body, concocted the story of the Resurrection and turned the message *of* Jesus into the message *about* Jesus.'[12] Or Jesus may have recovered and visited his disciples, showing them his wounds. If he lived he did not preach to the masses again, but kept a low profile away from the Romans and the Temple. Very few people understood what he was teaching anyway, so he may have given up, gone away and done something else. He took his message of the Kingdom (*enthousiasmos* – divinity within), the centre of love (*agape* – respect, understanding, honour, acceptance, trust, compassion, joy) with him. In its place we got a religion that focuses on sin, suffering, sacrifice, and salvation, with judgement at the end of life.

RESURRECTION

The physical resurrection of Jesus is central to Christian doctrine. Paul wrote 'If Christ has not been raised, your faith is futile and you are still in your sins' (1 Corinthians 15:17). Pagans had a god returning from the underworld – Dumuzi in Sumer, Tammuz in Babylonia and Adonis in Greece. In the east the gods died at the time of the summer drought and resurrection occurred when the drought ceased. Zoroastrians believed in a saviour who would initiate a general resurrection in the future. The Pharisees hoped for a promised Davidic Messiah and believed in the resurrection of the dead. To Paul, Jesus fulfilled the Old Testament prophecies and was the Messiah:

> Christ died for our sins, in accordance with the scriptures; that he was buried; that he was raised to life on the third day, according to the scriptures; that he appeared to Cephas [Peter], and afterwards to the Twelve. (1 Corinthians 15:3ff.)

In his letter to the Romans, written in 57 CE, Paul wrote:

> This gospel God announced beforehand in sacred scriptures through his prophets. It is about his Son: on the human level he was born of David's stock, but on the level of the spirit – the Holy Spirit – he was declared Son of God by a mighty act in that he rose from the dead: it is about Jesus Christ our Lord. (Romans 1:2ff.)

Paul's beliefs were carried into the Nicene Creed (see Appendix 2), which dates from 325 CE. The creed is accepted by the Roman Catholic, Eastern Orthodox, Anglican and other major Protestant denominations. When religious doctrines and creeds are followed dogmatically they can divide humanity into those who believe and those who do not – 'us' and 'them'. This attitude cosily bonds a family, tribe, religion or nation together in adversarial exclusivity. The need for an evil enemy is likely to lead to war against 'them'. Fighting on the side of what one believes to be right and good against what one believes to be wrong and bad gives meaning and purpose to life. Lawrence LeShan, who spent five years as a psychologist in the US Army, writes in his book *The Psychology of War* about fighting an enemy believed to be evil: 'The intensity of feeling in a war ... the engagement in a great crusade for a noble cause – all make our life more exciting and meaningful.'[13]

TODAY

With science, technology and education for all it is difficult for us to believe what our ancestors believed. When the 19th-century German philosopher Friedrich Nietzsche wrote 'God is dead' he was voicing the beliefs of many in the years to come. For some of us not only is the Old Testament Yahweh dead, but so is the New Testament God. Carl Jung was concerned that the removal of divinity from the world would leave a great hole in the human psyche, a hole that could be filled with dangerous 'isms', such as tribalism, authoritarianism, fundamentalism and patriotism. Jung considered isms 'the viruses of our day, and responsible for greater disasters than any medieval plague or pest has ever been'.[14] The followers of isms think they can 'save the world' with their beliefs, thus superficially giving a meaning and purpose to their lives. Alternatively, Jung's great hole in the human psyche may remain hopelessly empty, leading to ailments such as depression, which can be numbed by alcohol, drugs and other addictions, or to frantic searching for fulfilment by way of transient worldly accomplishments and acquisitions.

All through history humans have had thoughts of the divine. The Sumerians believed they were born of divinity and returned to her. Abraham left Sumer with his personal deity within him and handed him/her on to his offspring. Plato and Philo believed divinity resides within the soul and humans can reach that divinity, in fact yearn for direct experience of it. Jesus in the Gospel of Thomas said the kingdom is found within by knowing oneself, and so did the Gnostic, Monoimus. Meister Eckhart believed God is in the soul, and Carl Jung believed modern humanity is searching for that soul. Thomas Merton, the 20th-century American Roman Catholic priest/monk, said, 'The spiritual anguish of man has no cure but mysticism.'[15] Mysticism is found in all ages and all religions. Central to mysticism, wherever it is found, is acknowledgement of the divinity within. Such acknowledgement has universal results, beneficial to all mankind: it heals conflicts inside and out and ensures respect and understanding (love) for all. This is the supreme unity – wholeness, health and holiness – through which humanity becomes One.

MYSTICS

The intuitive mind is a sacred gift and the rational mind is a faithful servant. We have created a society that honors the servant and has forgotten the gift.
— Albert Einstein

The mystics' very personal inner divinity has often bewildered and frightened Western church leaders. In the 14th century, Meister Eckhart said the soul that knows divinity 'is in no need of sermons and teaching'. If this thought were to spread, the power and control of the Church would be threatened. Mystics have often been declared heretics – condemned as being among the 'them' whose beliefs lie outside the prescribed square of church doctrine. Despite this, mystics have continued their solitary, silent search for inner mysteries they know to be there. They find divinity by descending deeply into themselves. In 1990 Father Tissa Balasuriya published *Mary and Human Liberation*, in which he writes: '[Jesus] taught that the Spirit is in each human being, and that each has to respond to an inner call; there is no need of an external teacher.'[1] The Roman Catholic Church excommunicated Father Balasuriya in 1997 for his refusal to recant the alleged errors in his book, or to sign the profession of faith prepared for him by the Vatican.

It is noteworthy that the three words 'myth', 'mysticism' and 'mystery' are all derived from the Greek verb *musteion*, which means 'close the eyes or the mouth'. This indicates that all three words are rooted in an experience of darkness and silence. The 4th-century Christian mystic Evagrius Pontus – suspected by the Church of heresy – wrote that 'prayer means the shedding of thought'.[2] Beyond all worldly perceptions, beyond the busy inner thoughts of the rational, reasoning mind, there can be found another experience. When the conscious mind is stilled, the unconscious with its intuitions and wisdom can come into consciousness. Because this experience is indescribable in direct language, imaginative symbols such as those found in similes, metaphors, parables and myths have been used to describe it.

The union of the feminine darkness (Goddess/Mother/Earth/Nature/Soul/unconscious) with the masculine light (God/ Father/Heaven/Spirit/Intellect/conscious) in a sacred marriage creates the One from which all creation flows. This is Plato's 'at one with ourselves and with the gods'. It is the balance of yin and yang. It is Jesus' Kingdom. It is Jung's Wholeness. They all symbolically express the same thing using different imagery, words and practices.

Mystics of all ages and all religions have had similar experiences – their inner divinity is a unifying force, for 'unity is the very signature of the mystical'.[3] There are no 'us' and 'them' in mystical experience, but an overwhelming sense of the unity of all creation that is far beyond the sum of the parts. Perhaps the best-known example of this experience in the West is that of the layman St Francis of Assisi, who considered all nature the mirror of God. In mystical experience there is a 'love' (respect and understanding), and a deep-seated joy in life that pervades all. Rudolf Otto tried to explain this, though he knew it could be understood only by those who have the experience: 'It is a bliss … it gives the peace that passes understanding, and of which the tongue can only stammer brokenly. Only from afar, by metaphors and analogies, do we come to apprehend what it is in itself …'[4]

Lawrence LeShan asks the question, 'What is there in man that makes him so ready to go to war, in almost all cultures or economic conditions?' He points out that there are a few exceptions – the Quakers, Amish, Eskimo, California Mission Indians, Kalahari Bushmen – and raises the question of what factors these groups have in common.[5] Could it be that all these groups have a concept of inner divinity, through which they are aware of divinity within all others? Quakers, for example, believe in an Inward Light, divinity in everyone, an inner mystical Guide. Without creeds, clergy or outward sacraments their meetings are held in silence, and anyone who has an inner message to proclaim – man or woman – is welcome to do so and is listened to in silent respect. Over the years the Quakers have taken the lead in opposing slavery, brutality in prisons and insane asylums, oppression of women, militarism, and war. Today they are known for their pacifism and religious toleration.

The English mystical poet, Evelyn Underhill, helped to establish mystical theology as a respectable discipline. In the early 20th century she wrote:

> Reason has been trained to deal with the stuff of temporal existence. It will only make mincemeat of your experience of Eternity if you give it a chance; trimming, transforming, rationalising that ineffable vision, trying to force it into a symbolic system with which the intellect can cope. This is why

the great contemplatives utter again and again their solemn warning against the deceptiveness of thought when it ventures to deal with the spiritual intuitions of man.[6]

To still the interfering, rationalising intellect, Underhill used and recommended meditation; a meditation from her book *Practical Mysticism* appears in Appendix 3. The results of such meditation, she writes, are many:

A new suppleness has taken the place of that rigidity which you have been accustomed to mistake for strength of character: an easier attitude towards the accidents of life. Your whole scale of values has undergone a silent transformation, since you have ceased to fight for your own hand and regard the nearest-at-hand world as the only one that counts. You have become, as the mystics would say, 'free from inordinate attachments', the 'heat of having' does not scorch you any more; and because of this you possess great inward liberty, a sense of spaciousness and peace.[7]

Later in the 20th century Anthony de Mello, a Jesuit priest, said, 'Our violent spirituality has created problems for us.'[8] He wrote of an alternative: that we all have a mystical mind, 'a faculty which makes it possible for us to know God directly, to grasp and *intuit* him in his very being, though in a dark manner, apart from all thoughts, and concepts and images…' Ridding the mind of all thoughts, concepts and images exposes 'the emptiness, the darkness, the idleness, the nothingness' where the divine dwells. 'To silence the mind is an extremely difficult task. How hard it is to keep the mind from thinking, thinking, thinking, forever producing thoughts in a never-ending stream… You will be wise to use one thought to rid yourself of all the other thoughts that crowd into your mind. One thought, one image, one phrase or sentence or word that your mind can be made to fasten on.'[9] (This is the way Evelyn Underhill suggests in her meditation, Appendix 3.)

Father de Mello wrote that nobody can be said to have attained the pinnacle of Truth until a thousand sincere people have denounced him for blasphemy. He died in 1987, and ten years after his death the Vatican Congregation for the Doctrine of Faith condemned his work.

CARL GUSTAVE JUNG

Carl Jung has often been called a mystic, a term he disliked as he wanted to be regarded as a rational scientist. 'What the religious man calls God,' he said, 'is what the scientific intellect calls the collective unconscious.'[10] As a medical doctor, his research and conclusions have been taken seriously by the scientific world. He translated the ancient world of myths, mystery and mystics into modern psychological language which, for the first time, provides an explanation of the peace and compassion of the mystics.

Jung believed that when we are born our whole psyche is unconscious. According to Jung, the unconscious is the powerhouse that runs the body, keeping the heart beating, digestive system functioning and muscles moving in marvellous concert without any conscious effort. It also produces instincts (goading from within), intuitions (tuition from within), insight (sight from within), inspiration (the breath of the spirit from within). The word 'psyche' comes from a Greek word that means breath, life, soul – which are common to humans all over the world. From the psyche our cognitive consciousness develops – the rational, reasoning intellect with its limited capacity of attention and memory.* This consciousness has come to be considered our centre, a view which Jung rejected.

> The individual imagines that he has caught the psyche and holds her in the hollow of his hand. He is even making a science of her in the absurd supposition that the intellect, which is but a part and a function of the psyche, is sufficient to comprehend the much greater whole. In reality the psyche is the mother and the maker, the subject and even the possibility of consciousness itself. It reaches so far beyond the boundaries of consciousness that the latter could easily be compared to an island in the ocean.[11]

---

* In 1956 the American psychologist George Miller published a paper called 'The Magic Number Seven, Plus or Minus Two', in which he stated that the conscious mind can keep track of a maximum of only five to nine variables or pieces of information at one time. Cited in Joseph O'Connor and John Seymour, *Introducing Neuro-linguistic Programming*, p. 25.

Joseph Campbell puts the point bluntly in his book *The Power of Myth*:

> Consciousness thinks it is running the shop. But it's a secondary organ of a total human being, and it must not put itself in control. It must submit and serve the humanity of the body. When it does put itself in control, you get a man like Darth Vader in *Star Wars*, the man who goes over to the consciously intentional side.[12]

The wisdom that runs the body, the unconscious, is always there but ignored. Bringing it into consciousness will make us whole as human beings, and open our minds to deep-seated inherited, intuitive wisdom.

Jung takes dreams to be direct communications from the unconscious. When we sleep so does our intellect, allowing the unconscious to surface. We each have a personal unconscious that stores emotional problems, such as strained interpersonal relationships, which have been suppressed and ignored during the busy day. They make themselves known by way of dreams, which often indicate the solution. Jung believed our whole system is self-correcting and forward-looking. Some of our dreams can be disturbing, the shock of them penetrating consciousness and leaving a memory to be dealt with. When this happens, the unconscious, 'the mother and the maker', is then issuing a sharp warning. Should these warnings not be heeded then, as Bernie Siegel writes, 'you will become psychologically or spiritually troubled. And if that doesn't call your attention back to your path, your body will become physically ill.'[13] This is the way our personal daemon guides and directs us along the path of our personal myth.

There are dreams that shake the whole person when they occur. Such dreams often contain an archetype of the divinity. There is sometimes a voice, Jung says, an 'authoritative declaration or command, either of astonishing common sense and truth, or of profound philosophic allusion ... the voice shows an intelligence and a clarity superior to the dreamer's actual consciousness.'[14] These unforgettable dreams are so vivid they could more correctly be called 'visions'. If they are not religious experiences, they are very close to them.

Another kind of dream interested Jung:

...the kind of fantasy which comes to people when they are neither awake nor asleep, but in a state of reverie in which judgement is suspended but consciousness is not lost. Those who are familiar with the accounts given by creative people of how they happened upon their discoveries will recognise that it is in just this state of reverie that inspiration is most commonly reputed to occur.[15]

Jung called this process 'active imagination'. He encouraged his patients to express these 'waking' dreams, visions and fantasies artistically, in paintings, drawings, models, sculptures, poems, or song and dance, so as to discover hidden parts of themselves. 'The ability to reach a rich vein of material and translate it effectively into philosophy, literature, music, or scientific discovery is one of the hallmarks of what is commonly called genius.'[16]

That the unconscious is linked with creativity is attested by the fact that many creative people have described their creativity flowing from them with little or no conscious effort or control. For example,

- In 1862 the organic chemist Friedrich Kekulé dreamed of a whirling snake biting its tail, and from this his concept of the six-carbon benzene ring was born.
- Albert Einstein said that some of his theories, including the theory of relativity, came to him in a 'twilight' state.
- Robert Louis Stevenson had the plot of *Dr Jekyll and Mr Hyde* revealed to him in a dream.
- The children's writer Margaret Mahy said she puts the paper into the typewriter and the story writes itself.
- John Cleese said his comedy comes from his unconcious with little or no effort.
- When Bach was asked how he managed to think up all his new tunes, he is reported as saying, 'I have no need to think of them. I have the greatest difficulty not to step on them when I get out of bed in the morning.'
- Keith Richards tells the story of waking up in the middle of the night and putting something on tape. In the morning when he awoke and listened to the tape, there to his surprise was 30 seconds of a song the Rolling Stones later recorded to become the hit 'Satisfaction'.

Jazz musicians and many visual artists experience the same thing: turning off the conscious mind when working. All of these phenomena bypass the rational intellect, though expressing these unconscious revelations often involves the conscious mind – the part of the mind that has been taught how to organise and notate.

The study of such unconscious processes was virtually ignored by academic psychology until the 1970s. Up until then the focus of psychological research had been on external, observable behaviour and conscious mental processes. Today, psychologists are investigating not only dreams, trances and meditations, but such phenomena as sensory deprivation, mystical experiences, the effects of mind-altering drugs, parapsychology and shamanism.

Jung opened the doors to studying such phenomena more than 50 years ago, but only recently has academia ventured inside to investigate.

KNOW YOURSELF

Jung was concerned about the effect upon the psyche of what he called 'world despiritualization'.

> If the historical process of world despiritualization continues as hitherto, then everything of a divine or daemonic character outside us must return to the psyche, to the inside of the unknown man, whence it originally originated.[17]

Jung believed that the Hebrews projected inner divinity on to an outside God, and Christianity carried on the tradition by projecting it on to the God-man Jesus. With 'world despiritualization', our inborn divinity, if unrecognised, has to go somewhere. It is likely to be projected on to such objects as fantasy characters presented in movies, rock stars, sport stars and, most dangerously, religious and political leaders. The further we get away from our own inner divinity, our inner guides, the more susceptible we are to others influencing and leading us.

Just as we project divinity, so we project what Jung called the *shadow*, the unconscious part of our personality which, if ignored, rejected or despised by our conscious mind, is projected on to others. This causes us to see persons and things not as they are, but as we are. Jung calls such projections lies.

You can find them spread out in newspapers, in books, rumours, and ordinary social gossip. All gaps in our actual knowledge are still filled with projections. We are still so sure we know what other people think or what their true character is. We are convinced that certain people have all the bad qualities we do not know in ourselves or that they practise all those vices which could, of course, never be our own ... If you imagine someone who is brave enough to withdraw all these projections, then you get an individual who is conscious of a considerable shadow ... He is now unable to say that 'they' do this or that, 'they' are wrong, and that 'they' must be fought against ... Such a man knows that whatever is wrong in the world is in himself, and if he only learns to deal with his own shadow he has done something real for the world. He has succeeded in shouldering at least an infinitesimal part of the gigantic, unsolved social problems of our day. These problems are mostly so difficult because they are poisoned by mutual projections. How can anyone see straight when he does not even see himself and the darkness he unconsciously carries with him into all his dealings?[18]

Jung's concept of projection is echoed by other teachers. For example, Jesus in Matthew:

Why do you see the speck that is in your brother's eye, but do not notice the log that is in your own eye? ... You hypocrite, first take the log out of your own eye, and then you will see clearly to take the speck out of your brother's eye. (Matthew 7:1ff.)

Lawrence LeShan writing about war:

Projection is an extremely useful way to rid ourselves of intra-personal tensions. Instead of feeling bad about ourselves, we feel good as we go out to rid the world of evil. ...[19]

Jesus in Thomas:

(70) Jesus said: 'If You bring forth what is within You, what You have will save You. If You do not have that within You,

what You do not have within You will kill You.'
(111) ... Jesus says this: 'He who finds himself, the world is not worthy of him.'

The history of the world is filled with events that have come about not by logical, rational thinking, but because of irrational emotions, from the lust King David of Israel felt for the married woman Bathsheba, to the hatred of the Nazis for Jews. We know so little about the emotions that control our behaviour. In the words of Monoimus, 'Learn the sources of sorrow, joy, hate.' Some believe that all humanity is born with six basic emotions – anger, fear, disgust, sadness, surprise and happiness. How we learn to work with and understand these basic emotions determines our life and the life of our society.

TODAY

The Genesis creation myth is no longer serving us. We no longer need an authoritarian creator father devoid of refining female characteristics. Disobeying such a father is no longer considered the prime evil worthy of extreme punishment – this is a creation myth to control children. We have grown up, and know that we have many choices on a day-to-day basis. What we need is a guide to help us choose wisely.

Science – the new religion? – may have provided a new creation myth. It seems likely that we have evolved over millions of years. When our ancestors came down from the trees and started to walk upright they found their upper body, particularly their arms and hands, free to manipulate tools. They also became very vulnerable, and extra skills were required for survival. So the brain got larger with extra neurone connections, enabling these early humans to live and learn by their wits. And so cognitive consciousness developed. It sets us apart from other animals – we no longer rely solely on our instincts, although they are still there, but can make long-term plans, reason, learn complex languages, read and write, and make judgements regarding what is good and evil in the society we are born into. Such consciousness develops anew in every child; so each child needs to be taught those things considered important, including the mores of family and society. By contrast the unconscious is inherited and goes back millions of years; so it already has knowledge – as Meister Eckhart and Father Balasuriya state – and does not need external teaching. The more we concentrate on our linear thinking consciousness, however, the more we lose touch with the unconscious, the oldest, wisest part of us. Recognising that part, respecting it, and balancing it with our conscious mind is the modern-day challenge.

In mythological terms a story could be told which is very similar to Sumerian myths and beliefs. The Great Mother (the psyche, unconscious) produces a male counterpart (the intellect, cognitive consciousness) and a 'sacred marriage' takes place between them. As with all marriages this one may be either joyful, with mutual respect and understanding between the partners, or disruptive and unbalanced, with one partner having control and so creating conflict. How we manage the marriage within us determines our lives. If it is balanced we experience its sacredness.

At first, and along the way, we may need an external guide to encourage us and act as translator of the messages from within. Selection of this person is of paramount importance. He or she needs to have been along a similar path to the one you want to travel. The Greeks knew that only the wounded healer could heal, and he could heal only that which he had healed within himself.

Respecting any communication from the unconscious is where the search will begin. These communications may be as small as a 'slip of the tongue' or 'frog in the throat' when speaking; an emotion, image, word or song suddenly 'popping' into consciousness; a doodle drawn when the intellect is busily involved elsewhere. Or they may be as large as a horrific dream, an accident, a physical pain or illness. All such messages originate in the unconscious, the part of our mind that runs our body, stores our personal and inherited memories and produces our emotions. The unconscious is too powerful a force to ignore. From the recognition of her will come the union of the Sumerians' sacred marriage, the harmony of yin and yang, the recollected knowledge of Plato, the *enthousiasmos* of the Greeks, the wisdom of Proverbs, the love that Jesus displayed, the peace that passes understanding of Otto, and the Wholeness of Jung and Underhill.

The benefits are incalculable, ranging from physical and psychological health to wisdom and creativity. The promise is the meaning and purpose of a fulfilled life, a life that will be lived to its full potential.

> An ancient legend has it that when God was creating the world He was approached by four angels.
> The first one asked, 'How are you doing it?' – a scientist.
> The second, 'Why are you doing it?' – a philosopher.
> The third, 'Can I be of help?' – an altruist.
> The fourth, 'What is it worth?' – a merchant, trader.
> A fifth angel watched in wonder, and applauded in sheer delight. This one was the mystic.[20]

APPENDICES

APPENDIX ONE: THE GOSPEL OF (ACCORDING TO) THOMAS BY DIDYMUS JUDE THOMAS
TRANSLATED BY WIM VAN DEN DUNGEN, 1997

Here are the secret sayings which Jesus the Living spoke, and which Didymus Jude Thomas wrote down.

(1) And He said: "He who penetrates the meaning of these words will not taste death."

(2) Jesus said: "Let him who seeks not cease to seek until he finds: when he finds, he will become troubled. When he is troubled, he will wonder, and he will reign over the All."

(3) Jesus said: "If those who lead You say to You: 'See, the Kingdom is in heaven!' then the birds of the sky will be there before You. If they say to You, 'It is in the sea!' then the fish will be there before You. But the Kingdom is inside You and outside You. When You know yourselves, then You will be known, and You will know that You are the children of the Living Father. But if You do not know yourselves, then You dwell in poverty; then You are that poverty."

(4) Jesus said: "A person old in days will not hesitate to ask a child of seven days about the Place of Life, and he will live! For many who are first will become last, and they will become one and the same."

(5) Jesus said: "Know that what is before your face, and what is hidden from You will be revealed to You. For nothing hidden will fail to be revealed."

(6) His disciples asked and said to Him: "Do You want us to fast? How shall we pray and give alms? What diet shall we observe?"

Jesus said: "Tell no lie and do not what You hate, for all things are plain in the face of Heaven. For nothing hidden will fail to be revealed, and nothing covered will remain without being uncovered."

(7) Jesus said: "Fortunate is the lion which the man eats so that the lion becomes a man; and cursed is the man whom the lion eats so that the man becomes a lion."

(8) Then He said: "A man is like a wise fisherman who casts his net into the sea and drew it up from the sea full of small fish. Among them he found a fine large fish. The wise fisherman threw all the small fish back into the sea and chose the large fish without hesitation. He who has ears to hear, let him hear."

(9) Jesus said: "See, the sower went out, filled his hand, and scattered the seed. Some fell on the road; birds came and gathered them. Others fell on rocky ground, did not take root in the soil, and did not give ears of corn.

And others fell among thorns; they choked the seeds and worms ate them. And others fell on good soil and gave good fruit: it bore sixty per measure and a hundred and twenty per measure."

(10) Jesus said: "I have cast fire upon the world, and see, I watch over it until it blazes up."

(11) Jesus said: "This heaven will pass away, and the one above it will pass away. The dead are not alive, and the living will not die. In the days when You consumed death, You made death alive. When You come to dwell in the light, what will You do? On the day when You were one, You became two. But when You become two, what will You do?"

(12) The disciples said to Jesus: "We know that You will leave from us. Who is to be our leader?"

Jesus said to them: "From where you stand now, You are to go to James the Just, for whose sake heaven and earth came into being."

(13) Jesus said to His disciples: "Compare Me and tell Me whom I am like." Simon Peter said to Him: "You are like a righteous angel." Matthew said to Him: "You are like a wise philosopher." Thomas said to Him: "Master, my mouth is wholly incapable of saying to who You are like." Jesus said: "Your Master, because You have drunk, I am not; You have become intoxicated from the bubbling spring of living water which I have measured out." And He took him aside and spoke three words to him. When Thomas came back to his companions, they asked him: "What did Jesus say to You?" Thomas answered them: "If I tell You one of the words He said to me, You will take up stones and throw them at me and fire will come out of the stones and burn You."

(14) Jesus said to them: "If You fast, You will give rise to sin for yourselves; and if You pray, You will be condemned; and if You give alms, You will harm your spirit and when You enter any land and travel over the country, if they receive You, eat what they will set before You, and heal the sick among them. For what goes into your mouth will not defile You, but what comes out of your mouth will defile You."

(15) Jesus said: "When You see one who was not born of woman, prostrate yourselves on your faces and worship. That one is your Father."

(16) Jesus said: "Men think, perhaps, that it is peace which I have come to bring to the world. They do not know that I have come to bring to the earth: discord, fire, sword, and war. Indeed, if there are five in a house: three will be against two, and two against three, the father against the son, and the son against the father. And they will stand alone."

(17) Jesus said: "I shall give You what no eye has seen and what no ear has heard and what no hand has touched and what never arose in the heart of man."

(18) The disciples said to Jesus: "Tell us how our end will be." Jesus said: "So have You discovered the beginning, that You look for the end? For where the beginning is, there the end will be. Fortunate is he who stands at the beginning; he will know the end and will not taste death."

(19) Jesus said: "Fortunate is he who was before he became. If You become My disciples and listen to My words, these stones will serve You. For there are five trees for You in Paradise which remain unshaken summer and winter and their leaves do not fall. He who knows them will not taste death."

(20) The disciples said to Jesus: "Tell us what the Kingdom of Heaven is like." He said to them: "It is like a mustard seed, the smallest of all seeds. But when it falls on tilled soil, it produces a big plant and becomes a shelter for the birds of the sky."

(21) Mary said to Jesus: "To who are your disciples like?" He said: "They are like children who have settled in a field which is not theirs. When the owners of the field come, they will say: 'Let us have our field back.' When they will let them have the field back they will stand naked in their presence. Therefore I say to You, if the owner of a house knows that the thief is coming, he will stay awake till he comes and will not let him break in the house of his domain to carry away his goods. You, then, be on your guard against the world. Gird your loins with great strength so that the robbers find no way to come to You, for they will find the advantage which You expect. Let there be among You a smart man. When the fruit is ripe, he quickly came with his sickle in his hand and harvests it. He who has ears to hear, let him hear."

(22) Jesus saw infants being suckled. He said to His disciples: "These infants who suck are like those who enter the Kingdom." They said to Him: "Shall we then enter the Kingdom as infants?" Jesus said to them: "When You make the two one, and when You make the inside like the outside and the outside like the inside, and the above like the below, and when You make the male and the female one, so that the male will not be male nor the female female ; and when You fashion eyes in place of an eye, and a hand in place of a hand, and a foot in place of a foot, and a likeness in the place of a likeness; then will You enter the Kingdom."

(23) Jesus said: "I shall choose You, one from a thousand, and two from ten thousand, and they shall be as a single one."

(24) His disciples said to Him: "Show us the place where You are, since it is necessary for us to seek it." He said to them: "He who has ears, let him hear. There is light within a man of light, and he lights up the whole world. If he does not shine, there is darkness."

(25) Jesus said: "Love your brother like your own soul, watch over him like the apple of your eye."

(26) Jesus said: "You see the mote in your brother's eye, but You do not see the beam in your own eye. When You cast out the beam of your own eye, then You will see clearly enough to cast out the mote from your brother's eye."

(27) "If You do not fast as regards the world, You will not find the Kingdom. If You do not observe the Sabbath as Sabbath, You will not see the Father."

(28) Jesus said: "I took My place in the midst of the world, and I

appeared to them in flesh. I found them all drunk. I found none of them thirsty. And My soul ached for the sons of men, because they are blind in their heart and do not see that they came empty into the world, and empty they seek to leave it. But for the moment they are drunk. When they have slept off their wine, they will repent."

(29) Jesus said: "If the flesh came into being for the sake of the spirit, it is a wonder. But if the spirit came into being for the sake of the body, it is a wonder of wonders. Indeed, I marvel at how this great wealth has made its home in this poverty."

(30) Jesus said: "Where there are three gods, they are gods. Where there are two or one, I am with him."

(31) Jesus said: "No prophet is accepted in his own town; no physician heals those who know him."

(32) Jesus said: "A fortified city built on a high mountain cannot fall, nor can it be hidden."

(33) Jesus said: "Preach from your roof-tops that which You will hear in your ear. For no one lights a lamp and puts it under a bushel, nor does he put it in a hidden place, but rather he sets it on a lamp-stand so that all who come in and go out will see its light."

(34) Jesus said: "When a blind man leads another blind man both fall into a ditch."

(35) Jesus said: "It is not possible for anyone to enter the house of a strong man and take him by force unless he binds his hands; then one can ransack his house."

(36) Jesus said: "Do not be concerned from morning until evening and from evening until morning about what You will put on."

(37) His disciples said: "When will You reveal yourself to us and when will we see You?" Jesus said: "When You strip without being ashamed and take up your clothes and place them under your feet like little children and trample on them, then You will see the Son of the Living One, and You will not fear."

(38) Jesus said: "Often You have desired to hear these words which I am saying to You, and You have no one else to hear them from. There will be days when You will seek Me and will not find Me."

(39) Jesus said: "The Pharisees and the scribes have taken the keys of knowledge and hidden them. They have not entered, nor have they allowed those who wish so to enter. You, however, be as shrewd as serpents and as innocent as doves."

(40) Jesus said: "A vine shoot is planted away from the Father. Because it is not fastened, it will be plucked up from its roots and perish."

(41) Jesus said: "To him who has something will be given. And from him who has nothing will be taken away even the little he has."

(42) Jesus said: "Be passers-by."

(43) His disciples said to Him: "Who are You, that You say these things to us?"

Jesus said to them: "From what I say to You, You do not realize who I am. But You have become like the Jews, for they like the tree and hate its fruit and like the fruit and hate the tree!"

(44) Jesus said: "He who blasphemes against the Father will be forgiven, and he who blasphemes against the Son will be forgiven, but he who blasphemes against the Holy Spirit will not be forgiven either on earth or in heaven."

(45) Jesus said: "Grapes are not harvested from thorns, nor are figs gathered from thistles, for they do not give fruit. But someone good brings forth good things from his storehouse; someone evil brings forth evil things from the evil storehouse, which is in the heart, and says evil things. For if one's heart is filled with that, one brings forth evil things."

(46) Jesus said: "Among those born of women, from Adam until John the Baptist, there is none greater than John the Baptist that his eyes should not be lowered before him. Yet I have said, that if one of You becomes like a child he will know the Kingdom and be higher than John."

(47) Jesus said: "It is impossible for a man to mount two horses nor draw two bows. And it is impossible for a servant to serve two masters; otherwise, he will honor the one and insult the other. No man drinks old wine and desires at the same instant to drink new wine. And new wine is not put into old wineskins, lest they should burst; nor is old wine put into a new wineskin, lest it should spoil it. An old patch is not sown onto a new garment, for a tear would result."

(48) Jesus said: "When two make peace with each other in this one house, they will say to the mountain, 'Move!' and it will move."

(49) Jesus said: "Fortunate are You, the alone and the elect, for You will find the Kingdom. Because You came from it, You will also return to it again."

(50) Jesus said: "If they say to You, 'Where did You come from?' say to them: 'We came from the light, the place where the light came into being of itself established itself and revealed itself in their image. If they say to You: 'Who are You?' say: 'We are its sons. We are the elect of the Living Father.' If they ask You: 'What is the sign of your Father in You?' say to them: 'It is movement and rest.'

(51) His disciples said to Him: "On what day will the rest come to those who are dead, and on what day will the new world come?" He said to them: "What You expected has come, but You do not recognize it."

(52) His disciples said to Him: "Twenty-four prophets spoke in Israel, and all of them spoke about You." He said to them: "You have passed over the Living One who stands before You and have spoken of the dead."

(53) His disciples said to Him: "Is circumcision useful or not?" He said to them: "If it were useful, their Father would beget them already circumcised from their mother. Rather, the true circumcision in spirit is in all ways useful."

(54) Jesus said: "Fortunate are the poor, for yours is the Kingdom of Heaven."

(55) Jesus said: "He who does not hate his father and his mother cannot be My disciple. And he who does not hate his brothers and sisters and take up his cross as I do will not be worthy of Me."

(56) Jesus said: "He who has come to know the world has found a corpse, and he who has found a corpse, the world is not worthy of him."

(57) Jesus said: "The Kingdom of the Father is like a man who had good seed. His enemy came by night and sowed weeds among the good seed. The man did not allow them to pull out the weeds; he said to them : 'Do nothing ; so that You do not pull out the wheat along with the weeds.' For on the day of the harvest the weeds will be recognizable, and they will be pulled out and burnt."

(58) Jesus said: "Fortunate is the man who has suffered; he found Life."

(59) Jesus said: "Look to the Living One while You are alive, lest You die and then seek to see Him and are unable to see."

(60) They saw a Samaritan carrying a lamb on his way to Judea. He said to His disciples: "Why does that man carry the lamb around ?" They said to Him: "So that he may kill it and eat it." He said to them: "He will not eat it as long as it is alive, but only if he kills it and it has become a corpse." They said to Him: "He cannot do so otherwise." He said to them: "But You, seek for a place for yourselves to rest, lest You become a corpse and be eaten."

(61) Jesus said: "Two will rest on a bed: the one will die, and other will live." Salome said: "Who are You, man? You have taken a seat on my couch and have eaten at my table." Jesus said to her: "I am He who exists from the undivided. I was given some of the things of My Father." Salome said: "I am your disciple." Jesus said to her: "Therefore I say, if somebody is one, he will be full of light, but if he is divided, he will be full of darkness."

(62) Jesus said: "It is to those who are worthy of My mysteries that I tell My mysteries. Do not let your left hand know what your right hand is about to do."

(63) Jesus said: "There was a rich man who had a lot of money. He said: 'I shall put all my wealth to use so that I may sow, reap, plant, and fill my barn with harvest, with the result that I shall lack nothing.' Such were the thoughts of his heart, but during that night he died. He who has ears to hear, let him hear!"

(64) Jesus said: "A man had guests. And when he had prepared the dinner, he sent his servant to invite the guests. He went to the first one and said to him: 'My master invites You.' He said, 'I have claims against some merchants. They are coming to me this evening. I must go and give them my orders. I ask to be excused from the dinner.' He went to another and said to him: 'My master has invited You.' He said to him: 'I have just bought a house and am required for the day. I shall not have any spare time.' He went to another and said to him: 'My master invites You.' He said to him: 'My friend is going to get married, and I am to prepare the

banquet. I shall not be able to come. I ask to be excused from the dinner.' He went to another and said to him: 'My master invites You.' He said to him: 'I have just bought a farm, and I am on my way to collect the rent. I shall not be able to come. I ask to be excused.' The servant returned and said to his master: 'Those whom You invited to the dinner have asked to be excused.' The master said to his servant: 'Go out into the streets and those whom You happen to find, and bring in those that want to dine.' Buyers and merchants will not enter the places of My Father."

(65) He said: "There was an honorable man who owned a vineyard. He leased it to tenant farmers so that they might work it and he might collect the fruit from them. He sent his servant so that the tenants might give him the fruit of the vineyard. They seized his servant and beat him, all but killing him. The servant went back and told his master. The master said: 'Perhaps they did not recognize him.' He sent another servant. The tenants beat this one as well. Then the owner sent his son and said: 'Perhaps they will show respect to my son.' Because the tenants knew that he was the heir to the vineyard, they seized him and killed him. Let him who has ears hear."

(66) Jesus said: "Show Me the stone which the builders have rejected. It is the cornerstone."

(67) Jesus said: "He who believes to know the All but not himself falls completely short."

(68) Jesus said: "Fortunate are You when You are hated and persecuted. Where You were persecuted they will find no place."

(69) Jesus said: "Fortunate are those who are persecuted in their hearts. It is they who have truly come to know the Father. Fortunate are those who are hungry, for they will satisfy their bellies."

(70) Jesus said: "If You bring forth what is within You, what You have will save You. If You do not have that within You, what You do not have within You will kill You."

(71) Jesus said: "I will destroy this construction, and no one will be able to rebuild it again."

(72) A man said to Him: "Tell my brothers to divide my father's possessions with me." He said to him: "Man, who has made Me a divider?" He turned to His disciples and said to them: "I am not a divider, am I?"

(73) Jesus said: "The harvest is great but the labourers are few. Pray the Lord to send out labourers for the harvest."

(74) He said: "Lord, many are around the water-spring but nobody is in the well."

(75) Jesus said: "Many stand outside at the door, but it is the solitaries who will enter the bridal chamber."

(76) Jesus said: "The Kingdom of the Father is like a man, a merchant, who owned goods and discovered a pearl. This merchant was clever. He sold the merchandise and bought the pearl alone. You also seek his enduring treasure where no moth comes near to eat and no worm destroys."

(77) Jesus said: "I am the Light that falls on all things. I am the All.

From Me the All has gone out and to Me the All came back. Cleave a piece of wood, and I am there. Lift up a stone, and You will find Me there."

(78) Jesus said: "Why did You go out into the desert? To see a reed shaken by the wind? To see a man clothed in fine garments? Your kings and your great men are the ones clothed in fine garments, and they are not able to know the truth."

(79) A woman from the crowd said to Him: "Fortunate is the womb which bore You and the breasts which fed You." He said to her: "Fortunate are those who have heard the Word of the Father and kept it. For days are coming when You will say: 'Fortunate the womb that has not conceived and the breasts which have not given suck.'

(80) Jesus said: "He who knew the world has mastered the body, but he who has mastered the body is superior to the world."

(81) Jesus said: "He who has grown wealthy will rule, and he who possesses power will renounce it."

(82) Jesus said: "Whoever is near Me is near the fire, and whoever who is far from Me is far from the Kingdom."

(83) Jesus said: "Images are visible to man, and the light which is in them is hidden in the image of the Light of the Father. He will reveal Himself and His image is hidden by His light."

(84) Jesus said: "When You see your own likeness, You rejoice. But when You see the images of yourselves which came into being before You, which do not die nor become visible, how much then will You be able to bear?"

(85) Jesus said: "Adam came into being from a great power and a great wealth, and he did not become worthy of You. For had he been worthy of You, he would not have experienced death."

(86) Jesus said: "The foxes have their holes and the birds have their nests, but the Son of Man has no place to lay his head and rest."

(87) Jesus said: "Wretched is the body which depends on a body, and wretched is the soul dependent on these two."

(88) Jesus said: "The angels and the prophets will come to You and give You what is yours. You, give them what is in your hands, and ask yourselves: 'On which day will they come to receive what is theirs?'

(89) Jesus said: "Why do You wash the outside of the cup? Do You not realize that He who made the inside is the same one who made the outside?"

(90) Jesus said : "Come to Me, for My yoke is easy and My Lordship is mild, and You will find rest for yourselves."

(91) They said to Him: "Tell us who You are so that we may believe in You." He said to them: "You examine the face of the sky and of the earth, but You have not recognized He who stands in front of You, and You do not know how to examine this moment."

(92) Jesus said: "Seek and You will find. Yet, what You asked Me about in former times and which I did not tell to You then, I now desire to tell You, but You do not ask after it."

(93) "Do not give what is holy to the dogs, lest they throw it on the dunghill. Do not cast pearls to swine, lest they grind them [to bits]."

(94) Jesus said: "He who seeks will find, and he who knocks will be let in."

(95) Jesus said: "If You have money, do not lend it at interest, but give it to someone from whom You will not get it back."

(96) Jesus said: "The Kingdom of the Father is like a woman who put a little yeast in some flour, and made some big loaves with it. He who has ears, let him hear!"

(97) Jesus said: "The Kingdom of the Father is like a woman who was carrying a jar full of meal. While she was walking on a far road the handle of the jar broke and the meal emptied out behind her on the road. She did not realize it. She had noticed no accident. When she reached her house, she put the jar down and found it empty."

(98) Jesus said: "The Kingdom of the Father is like a man who wanted to kill a powerful man. In his own house he drew his sword and stuck it into the wall in order to find out whether his hand would be firm enough. Then he slew the powerful man."

(99) The disciples said to Him: "Your brothers and your mother are standing outside." He said to them: "Those here who do the will of My Father are My brothers and My mother. It is they who will enter the Kingdom of My Father."

(100) They showed Jesus a gold coin and said to Him: "Caesar's men demand taxes from us." He said to them: "Give Caesar what belongs to Caesar, give Elohim what belongs to Elohim, and give Me what is Mine."

(101) "He who does not hate his father and his mother as I do cannot become a disciple to Me. And he who does not love his father and his mother as I do cannot become a disciple to Me. For My mother [gave Me death], but My true Mother gave Me life."

(102) Jesus said: "Damn the Pharisees, for they are like a dog sleeping in the manger of oxen, for neither does he eat nor does he let the oxen eat."

103) Jesus said: "Fortunate is the man who knows where the robbers are going to enter, so that he may get up, gather his [house], and girds his loins before they enter."

(104) They said to Jesus : "Come, let us pray and fast." Jesus said: "What then is the sin that I have committed, or wherein have I been at fault? But when the bridegroom leaves the bridal chamber, then let them fast and pray."

(105) Jesus said: "He who knows his father and mother will he be called son of a harlot?"

(106) Jesus said: "When You make the two one, You will become Sons of Man, and if You say: 'Mountain, move !', it will move."

(107) Jesus said: "The Kingdom is like a shepherd who had a hundred sheep. One of them, the largest, went astray. He left the ninety-nine and looked for that single sheep until he found it. When he had gone to such

trouble, he said to the sheep: 'I love You more than the ninety-nine.'

(108) Jesus said: "He who will drink from My mouth will become like Me. I myself shall become like him, and the hidden will be revealed to him."

(109) Jesus said: "The Kingdom is like a man who had a treasure hidden in his field without knowing it. And after he died, he left it to his son. The son did not know about the treasure. He accepted the field and sold it. And the one who bought it went plowing and found the treasure. He began to lend money at interest to those who wanted it."

(110) Jesus said: "He who has found the world and become rich, let him renounce the world."

(111) Jesus said: "The heavens and the earth will be rolled up before You. And whoever is living from the Living One will not see death." Jesus says this: "He who finds himself, the world is not worthy of him."

(112) Jesus said: "Damn the flesh that depends on the soul; damn the soul that depends on the flesh."

(113) His disciples said to Him: "When will the Kingdom come?" Jesus said: "It does not come by expecting it. It will not be a matter of saying: 'See, it is here!' or: 'Look, it is there!' Rather, the Kingdom of the Father is spread over the earth and men do not see it."

(114) Simon Peter said to them: "Let Mary leave us, for women are not worthy of life." Jesus said: "Look, I will guide her in order to make her male, so that she too may become a living spirit like You males. For every female who will make herself male will enter the Kingdom of Heaven."*

Dungen, van den, W.: "The Gospel of Thomas", in: Webpublications of Sophia, Society for Philosophy, Antwerp, Reg.N°18, 1997, URL: http://www.sofiatopia.org/equiaeon/thomas.htm.

---

* Professor Helmut Koester suggests that Jesus meant the '"maleness" of the solitary existence.' Others believe this saying was added at a later date. It appears to be from the writings of Philo of Alexandria: 'Progress is indeed nothing else than the giving up of the female gender by changing into the male …'. It does not fit with what Jesus taught and did. (For Helmut Koester's quote see the Introduction to *The Gospel of Thomas* in Robinson, *The Nag Hammadi Library* p. 126. For Philo's quote see *The Feminine Dimension of the Divine* by Joan C. Engelsman, cited in *The Myth of the Goddess*, p. 614.)

APPENDIX TWO: THE NICENE CREED

We believe in one God,
the Father, the Almighty,
maker of heaven and earth,
of all that is seen and unseen.
We believe in one Lord, Jesus Christ,
the only Son of God,
eternally begotten of the Father,
God from God, Light from Light,
true God from true God,
begotten, not made, one in Being with the Father.
Through him all things were made.
For us men and for our salvation
he came down from heaven:
by the power of the Holy Spirit
he was born of the Virgin Mary, and became man.
For our sake he was crucified under Pontius Pilate;
he suffered, died, and was buried.
On the third day he rose again
in fulfilment of the Scriptures;
he ascended into heaven
and is seated on the right hand of the Father.
He will come again in glory
to judge the living and the dead,
and his kingdom will have no end.
We believe in the Holy Spirit, the Lord, the giver of life,
who proceeds from the Father and the Son.
With the Father and the Son he is worshipped and glorified.
He has spoken through the Prophets.
We believe in one holy catholic and apostolic Church.
We acknowledge one baptism for the forgiveness of sins.
We look for the resurrection of the dead,
and the life of the world to come. Amen.

APPENDIX THREE: MEDITATION

Take, then, an idea, an object, from amongst the common stock, and hold it before your mind. The selection is large enough: all sentient beings may find subjects of meditation to their taste, for there lies a universal behind every particular of thought, however concrete it may appear, and within the most rational propositions the meditative eye may glimpse a dream.

> Reason has moons, but moons not hers
> Lie mirror'd on her sea,
> Confounding her astronomers
> But, O delighting me.

Even those objects which minister to our sense-life may well be used to nourish our spirits too. Who has not watched the intent meditations of a comfortable cat brooding upon the Absolute Mouse? You, if you have a philosophic twist, may transcend such relative views of Reality, and try to meditate on Time, Succession, even Being itself: or again on human [communication], birth, growth, and death, on a flower, a river, the various tapestries of the sky. Even your own emotional life will provide you with the ideas of love, joy, peace, mercy, conflict, desire. You may range, with Kant, from the stars to the moral law. If your turn be to religion, the richest and most evocative of fields is open to your choice; from the plaster image to the mysteries of Faith.

But, the choice made, it must be held and defended during the time of meditation against all invasions from without, however insidious their encroachments, however "spiritual" their disguise. It must be brooded upon, gazed at, seized again and again, as distractions seem to snatch it from your grasp. A restless boredom, a dreary conviction of your own incapacity, will presently attack you. This, too, must be resisted at sword-point. The first quarter of an hour thus spent in attempted meditation will be, indeed, a time of warfare: which should at least convince you how unruly, how ill-educated is your attention, how miserably ineffective your will, how far away you are from the captaincy of your own soul. It should convince, too, the most common-sense of philosophers of the distinction between real time, the true stream of duration which is life, and the sequence of seconds so carefully measured by the clock. Never before has the stream flowed so slowly, or fifteen minutes taken so long to pass. Consciousness has been lifted to a longer, slower rhythm, and is not yet adjusted to its solemn march.

But, striving for this new poise, intent on the achievement of it, presently it will happen to you to find that you have indeed – though you know not how – entered upon a fresh plane of perception, altered your relation with things.

First, the subject of your meditation begins, as you surrender to its influence, to exhibit unsuspected meaning, beauty and power. A perpetual growth of significance keeps pace with the increase of attention which you bring to bear on it; that attention which is the agent of all your apprehensions, physical and mental alike. It ceases to be thin and abstract. You sink as it were into the deeps of it, rest in it, "unite" with it; and learn in this still, intent communion, something of its depth and breadth and height, as we learn by direct (communication) to know our friends.

… And gradually, you will come to be aware of an entity, a You, who can thus hold at arm's length, be aware of, look at, an idea – a universe – other than itself.… This is the first step upon the ladder which goes – as the mystics would say – from "multiplicity to unity," you have to some extent withdrawn yourself from that union with unrealities, with notions and concepts, which has hitherto contented you; and at once all the values of existence are changed. …

… You will at last discover that there is something within you – something behind the fractious, conflicting life of desire – which you can recollect, gather up, make effective for new life. You will, in fact, know your own soul for the first time. …

So, in a measure, you have found yourself: have retreated behind all that flowing appearance, that busy, unstable consciousness with its moods and obsessions, its feverish alternations of interest and apathy, its conflicts and irrational impulses, which even the psychologists mistake for You. Thanks to this recollective act, you have discovered in your inmost sanctuary a being not wholly practical, who refuses to be satisfied by your busy life of correspondences with the world of normal men, and hungers for communion with a spiritual universe. And this thing so foreign to your surface consciousness, yet familiar to it and continuous with it, you recognise as the true Self.

Evelyn Underhill, *Practical Mysticism*, pp. 26–7.

ENDNOTES

Myths
1. Plato, *Republic*, Book X, cited in James Hillman, *The Soul's Code*, p. 8.
2. C. G. Jung, *Collected Works*, vol. 17, paras. 284–323, cited in *The Essential Jung*, selected and introduced by Anthony Storr, pp. 199, 200.
3. Bernie Siegel, *Peace, Love and Healing*, pp. 49–50.
4. Letter to M. R. Braband-Isaac, 22 July 1939. In Gerhard Adler and Aniela Jaffe eds., *C. G. Jung: Letters*, , vol. 1, pp. 274–5, cited in Anne Baring and Jules Cashford, *The Myth of the Goddess*, p. 681.
5. Ibid.
6. Joseph L. Henderson, 'Ancient Myths and Modern Man'. In Carl G. Jung. ed., *Man and his Symbols*, p. 98.
7. C. G. Jung, 'The Psychology of the Child Archetype'. In C. G. Jung and C. Kerényi, eds., *Essays on a Science of Mythology*, p. 71.
8. Marie-Louise von Franz, *The Interpretation of Fairy Tales*, Ch V.

Sumer
1. This abridged summary of the myth is based on Joseph Campbell, *Oriental Mythology*, p. 108; Baring and Cashford, *The Myth of the Goddess*, p. 187; and Thorkild Jacobsen, *The Treasures of Darkness*, p. 113.
2. S. N. Kramer, *From the Poetry of Sumer*, pp. 29–30, cited in Baring and Cashford, *The Myth of the Goddess*, pp. 670, 671.
3. Mircea Eliade, *The Two and the One*, pp. 122 ff.
4. David Bohm, *Wholeness and the Implicate Order*, p. xi.
5. As in No. 1, above.
6. Joseph Campbell, *Occidental Mythology*, p. 7.
7. Donald A. Mackenzie, *Myths of Babylonia and Assyria*, pp. 16–17.
8. von Franz, *The Interpretation of Fairy Tales*, Ch. VII.

9. This abridged summary of the myth is based on John Gray, *Near Eastern Mythology*, pp. 9, 10; Campbell, *Occidental Mythology*, p. 106; and Baring and Cashford, *The Myth of the Goddess*, p. 432.
10. Karen Armstrong, *A History of God*, p. 27.
11. Baring and Cashford, *The Myth of the Goddess*, p. 430.
12. Jacobsen, *The Treasures of Darkness*, p. 77.
13. Baring and Cashford, *The Myth of the Goddess*, p. 171 and Gray, *Near Eastern Mythology*, pp. 55, 56.
14. Campbell, *Occidental Mythology*, p. 80.
15. Mackenzie, *Myths of Babylonia and Assyria*, pp. 228, 229.

Babylonia
1. This abridged summary of the myth is based on Campbell, *Occidental Mythology*, pp. 76ff.; Baring and Cashford, *The Myth of the Goddess*, pp. 76ff.; Jacobsen, *The Treasures of Darkness*, pp. 168ff. and Gray, *Near Eastern Mythology*, pp. 33, 35.
2. Jacobsen, *The Treasures of Darkness*, pp. 80–1.
3. Campbell, *Occidental Mythology*, p. 86.
4. C. G. Jung, cited in Baring and Cashford, *The Myth of the Goddess*, p. 299.
5. Jacobsen, *The Treasures of Darkness*, p. 158 (Surpu Tablets v–vi, lines 11–12).
6. Ibid., p. 159.

Abraham and his Descendants
1. Cf. Otto Rank, *Der Mythus von der Geburt des Helden*. Cited in Campbell, *Occidental Mythology*, pp. 73–4.
2. Rudolf Otto, *The Idea of the Holy*, p. 73.
3. Baring and Cashford, *The Myth of the Goddess*, p. 48.
4. Marija Gimbutas, *The Goddesses and Gods of Old Europe*, p. 196.
5. Baring and Cashford, *The Myth of the Goddess*, p. 513.
6. Ibid., p. 448.
7. Campbell, *Occidental Mythology*, pp. 21, 22.
8. C. G. Jung, *Letters*, vol. 2, p. 434, cited in Baring and Cashford, *The Myth of the Goddess*, pp. 441, 442.
9. Summary adapted from Maneckji Nusservanji Dhalla, *History of Zoroastrianism*, pp. 312ff.

Jesus

1. Armstrong, *A History of God*, p. 97.
2. Mackenzie, *Myths of Babylonia and Assyria*, p. 236.
3. Ibid., p. 46.
4. Otto, *The Idea of the Holy*, p. 64.
5. Armstrong, *A History of God*, p. 83.
6. Thomas Cahill, *Desire of the Everlasting Hills*, pp. 69–70.
7. Introduction by Helmut Koester to the translation of *The Gospel of Thomas* in J. M. Robinson, ed., *The Nag Hammadi Library*, pp. 124–5.
8. Elaine Pagels, *The Gnostic Gospels*, p. 16.
9. Letter to Theophrastus, quoted by Hyppolytus of Rome in *The Refutation of All Heresies*, Book VIII, cited in Pagels, *The Gnostic Gospels*, p. 21.
10. Matthew Fox, *Meditations with Meister Eckhart*, p. 3.
11. Ibid., p. 28.
12. Cited in Robert K. C. Forman, *Meister Eckhart*, p. 110.
13. Ibid., p. 96.
14. Ibid., p. 211.
15. Stephen R. L. Clark, in Anthony Kenny, ed., *The Oxford Illustrated History of Western Philosophy*, pp. 26–7.

Christianity

1. Campbell, *Occidental Mythology*, pp. 113–14.
2. Stewart Perowne, *The Life and Time of Herod the Great*, p.141.
3. Ibid.
4. Cf.. the testimony of Theodore Parker quoted in William James, *Varieties of Religious Experience*, p. 81, cited in Otto, *The Idea of Holy*, p. 53.
5. *Enchyridion* 26.27, cited in Armstrong, *A History of God*, pp. 144, 145.
6. Henry Betterson, ed., *Documents of the Christian Church*, p. 213, cited in Baring and Cashford, *The Myth of the Goddess*, pp. 533, 534.
7. Matthew Fox, *Original Blessing*, p. 51.
8. *On Female Dress*, I, I., cited in Armstrong, *A History of God*, p. 145.
9. Pagels, *The Gnostic Gospels*, pp. 81ff.
10. Campbell, *Oriental Mythology*, p. 10.
11. Gray, *Near Eastern Mythology*, p. 126.

12. Lloyd Geering, *The World to Come*, p. 42.
13. Lawrence LeShan, *The Psychology of War*, p. 95.
14. Laurens van der Post, *Jung: and the Story of our Time*, p. 4.
15. Thomas Merton, *The New Man*, p. 66.

Mystics
1. Tissa Balasuriya, *Mary and Human Liberation*, p. 82.
2. John Macquarrie, *Thinking about God*, p. 34, cited in Armstrong, *A History of God*, p. 255.
3. Otto, *The Idea of the Holy*, p. 104.
4. Ibid., pp. 33–4.
5. LeShan, *The Psychology of War*, pp. 108, 109.
6. Evelyn Underhill, *Practical Mysticism*, p. 42.
7. Ibid., p. 39.
8. Anthony de Mello, *The Song of the Bird* (back cover).
9. Anthony de Mello, *Sadhana*, pp. 29, 32–3.
10. Ronald Hayman, *A Life of Jung*, p. 4.
11. Storr, ed., *The Essential Jung*, p. 243.
12. Joseph Campbell, *The Power of Myth*, p. 146.
13. Siegel, *Peace, Love and Healing*, pp. 49–50.
14. C. G. Jung, *Psychology and Religion*, pp. 45, 49.
15. Anthony Storr, *C. G. Jung*, p. 110.
16. C. G. Jung, *Man and his Symbols*, p. 25.
17. Storr, ed., *The Essential Jung*, p. 244.
18. Ibid., pp. 242–3.
19. LeShan, *The Psychology of War*, p. 77.
20. Anthony de Mello, *The Prayer of the Frog*, p. 6.

BIBLIOGRAPHY

Armstrong, Karen. *A History of God*. London: Heinmann, 1993.

Balasuriya, Tissa. *Mary and Human Liberation*. Valley Forge: Trinity Press International, 1997.
Baring, Anne, and Jules Cashford. *The Myth of the Goddess*. London and New York: Arkana, 1993.
Becker, Ernest. *The Denial of Death*. New York: The Free Press, 1975.
Blake, William. *Songs of Innocence and Experience*. New York: Dover, 1992.
Book of Common Prayer. London: Ebury, 1992.
Boyce, Mary. *Zoroastrians*. London: Routledge & Kegan Paul, 1979.
Bradley, Ian. *Marching to the Promised Land*. London: J. Murray, 1992.
Brown, Dan. *The Da Vinci Code*. New York: Doubleday, 2003.

Cahill, Thomas. *Desire of the Everlasting Hills*. Oxford: Lion Publishing, 2002.
Campbell, Joseph. *The Mythic Image*. Princeton: Princeton University Press, 1990.
——— *The Masks of God: Occidental Mythology, Oriental Mythology, Creative Mythology*. Harmondsworth: Arkana, 1991.
——— with Bill Moyes, ed. Betty Sue Flowers. *The Power of Myth*. New York: Doubleday, 1988.
Cornwell, John. *Breaking Faith*. New York: Viking Compass, 2001.

de Mello, Anthony. *The Prayer of the Frog*. Anand: Gujarat Sahitya Prakash, 1991.
——— *The Song of the Bird*. Anand: Gujarat Sahitya Prakash, 1987.
——— *Sadhana*. New York: Image Books, 1984.
——— *The Way to Love*. New York: Image Books, 1991.
Dhalla, Maneckji Nusservanji. *History of Zoroastrianism*. New York: AMS Press, 1965.
Diamant, Anita, *The Red Tent*. Crows Nest, NSW: Allen & Unwin, 1998.

Eliade, Mircea. *The Two and the One*. London: Harvill Press, 1965.
———. *World Religions*. San Francisco: Harper, 1991.

Faraday, Ann. *Dream Power*. London: Hodder and Stoughton, 1972.

———— *The Dream Game*. New York: Harper & Rowe, 1976.
Feinstein, David, and Stanley Krippner. *The Mythic Path*. Los Angeles: Tarcher, 1997.
Ferris, Paul. *Dr Freud*. London: Sinclair-Stevenson, 1997.
Forman, Robert K. C. *Meister Eckhart*. Shaftesbury and Rockport: Element, 1991.
Foundation for Inner Peace, *A Course in Miracles*. Glen Allen, CA: The Foundation for Inner Peace, 1992.
Fox, Matthew. *Original Blessing*. Santa Fe: Bear, 1983.
———— *Meditations with Meister Eckhart*. Santa Fe: Bear, 1983.
———— *Meister Eckhart*. Rochester: Inner Traditions, 2000.
Frazer, James. *The Golden Bough*. London: Chancellor Press, 2000.
Funk, Robert W., Roy W. Hoover, and the Jesus Seminar. *The Five Gospels*. New York: Macmillan International, 1993.

Garfield, Leon, and Edward Blishen. *The God Beneath The Sea*. London: Longman, 1970.
Geering, Lloyd. *The World to Come*. Wellington: Bridget Williams, 1999.
———— *Tomorrow's God*. Wellington: Bridget Williams, 1994.
Gimbutas, Marija. *The Living Goddess*. Berkeley: University of California Press, 1999.
Goldhill, Simon. *The Temple of Jerusalem*. London: Profile, 2004.
Gray, John. *Near Eastern Mythology*. New York: Peter Bedrick, 1982.

Hay, Louise. *You Can Heal Your Life*. Santa Monica: Hay House, 1987.
Hayman, Ronald. *A Life of Jung*. London: Bloomsbury, 1997.
Higgins, Michael W. *Heretic Blood*. Toronto: Stoddart, 1998.
Hillman, James. *The Soul's Code*. New York: Random House, 1996.
———— *The Dream and the Underworld*. New York: Perennial Library, 1979.

Jacobsen, Thorkild. *The Treasures of Darkness*. New Haven and London: Yale University Press, 1976.
Johnson, Buffie. *Lady of the Beasts*. Rochester, Vt.: Inner Traditions, 1994.
Johnson, Paul. *A History of the Jews*. London: Orion, 1993.
Jung, Carl G. *Man and His Symbols*. London: Aldus in association with W.H. Allen, 1964.
————*Memories, Dreams, Reflections*. London: Routledge and Collins, 1963.
————*Psychology and Religion*. New Haven and London: Yale University Press, 1966
————and C. Kerényi, eds., *Essays on a Science of Mythology*. Princeton: Princeton University Press, 1978.

Kenny, Anthony, ed. *The Oxford Illustrated History of Western Philosophy*. Oxford: Oxford University Press, 1994.

LeShan, Lawrence. *The Psychology of War*. New York: Helios Press, 2002.
Llosa, Mario Vargas. *The Storyteller*. London: Faber, 1989.
The Lion Handbook to the Bible. Oxford: Lion, 1983.

Mackenzie, Donald A. *Myths of Babylonia and Assyria*. London: Gresham, n.d.
Market, Christopher. *I Ching*. Wellingborough, England: Aquarian Press, 1986.
Merton, Thomas. *The New Man*. New York: Bantam Books, 1961.

O'Connor, Joseph, and John Seymour. *Introducing Neuro-Linguistic Programming*. London and San Francisco: Aquarian/Thorsons, 1993.
O'Dea, Thomas F. *The Mormons*. Chicago, London: The University of Chicago Press, 1957.
Otto, Rudolf. *The Idea of the Holy*. London and New York: Oxford University Press, 1950.

Pagels, Elaine. *The Gnostic Gospels*. London: Weidenfeld and Nicolson, 1980.
Perowne, Stewart. *The Life and Times of Herod the Great*. Hodder and Staughton Ltd, 1956.

Reade, Julian. *Mesopotamia*. London: British Museum, 2000.
Rifkin, Ira, ed. *Spiritual Innovators*. Woodstock, Vt.: Skylight Path, 2002.
Robinson, J. M., ed. *The Nag Hammadi Library*. San Francisco: Harper SanFrancisco, 1990.
Rossi, Ernest Lawrence. *The Symptom Path to Enlightenment*. Pacific Palisades: Palisades Gateway, 1996.
Russell, Bertrand. *History of Western Philosophy*. London: George Allen and Unwin, 1948.

Schultz, Duane. *Intimate Friends, Dangerous Rivals*. Los Angeles: J. P. Tarcher, 1990.
Siegel, Bernie S. *Love, Medicine and Miracles*. New York: Harper & Row, 1986.
———. *Peace, Love and Healing*. New York: Harper & Row, 1989.
Smith, Huston. *The World's Religions*. San Francisco: HarperSanFrancisco, 1991.
Storr, Anthony. *C. J. Jung*. New York: Viking Press, 1973.
———. *The Essential Jung*. Princeton: Princeton University Press, 1983.
———. *The Integrity of the Personality*. Oxford: Oxford University Press, 1992.

———— *Feet of Clay*. London: HarperCollins, 1997.
Sykes, Bryan. *The Seven Daughters of Eve*. London: Bantam, 2001.

Time-Life Books. *Lost Civilization: The Holy Land*. Alexandria, Va.: Time-Life Books, 1992.
————*Lost Civilization: Sumer: Cities of Eden*. Alexandria, Va.: Time-Life Books, 1993.

Underhill, Evelyn. *Practical Mysticism*. Mineola, NY: Dover Publications, 2000.

van der Post, Laurens. *Jung and the Story of our Time*. New York: Random House, 1976.
Vipont, Elfrida. *George Fox and the Valiant Sixty*. London: Hamilton, 1973.
von Franz, Marie-Louise. *The Interpretation of Fairy Tales*. E. Lancing: Shambhala, 1996.

Walker, Barbara G. *The Woman's Encyclopaedia of Myths and Secrets*. San Francisco: Harper, 1983.
Wangerin, Walter. *The Book of God*. Oxford: Lion, 1996.
Wilson, A N. *Paul*. London: Sinclair-Stevenson, 1997.

INDEX

Abraham 5, 11, 21, 24, 30, 37, 46, 49–51, 98, 126
Accident Compensation Corporation 15
active imagination 105
Adam 4, 20, 35, 54, 86, 88–90, 93, 116, 119
Aegean Sea 52, 57, 62
agape 20, 96
Ahura Mazda 63–64
Akkadia 40, 53
Akki 37
Alexander the Great 48, 62–63, 66–67
Alexandria 74–76, 121, 132
Amish 101
Amorites 38, 40
Anath 52
Anglican Book of Common Prayer 92
Angra Mainyu 64
Apsu 42
Aramaic 62
archetypes 19, 45
Armstrong, Karen 73, 76, 126, 129
artists 106
Asclepius 8, 32, 74
Asherah 52
Ashoreth 34
Assyrians 58–60, 65
Astarte 52–53
Astyages 63
atonement 76, 88, 90
Augustine 81, 89–90
Axis of Evil 38

Baal 52
Babel 26, 50
Babylon 11, 40, 43, 47–48, 61–62, 65, 67, 69
Babylonian Empire 8, 40, 47–48
Bach 105, 62
Balasuriya, Tissa 100, 128–129
Baring, Anne 7–8, 125, 129
Benjamin 58, 65
Bethlehem 94–95
blasphemy 46, 79, 102
blood 26, 43, 54, 86–88, 130, 53, 94, 120, 156, 194

Bohm, David 28, 125
Buddha 94
Bush, George W. 38

Cahill, Thomas 77, 127, 129
Cain and Abel 35, 50
Calvin, John 90
Campbell, Joseph 11, 13, 27, 29, 33, 37–38, 44, 83, 93, 103–104, 125, 128–129
Canaan 20–21, 27, 37, 50, 52–53, 55–56
Cashford, Jules 54, 125, 129
Celsus 74
Chaldeans 11, 60
Christianity 5, 11, 20–21, 37, 45, 47, 64–66, 68, 74, 76, 80–81, 84–86, 90–91, 93, 106, 127, 55
Cicero 74
Code of Hammurabi 39, 92–93
cognitive consciousness 103, 108–109
collective myths 19, 103
collective unconscious 19, 44, 103
consciousness 16, 18, 34, 45, 66, 83, 100, 103–105, 108–109, 123–124
Consciousness Research 16
creation myths 12, 19–21, 24–25, 54
creativity 45, 105, 109
Crete 9, 11, 30, 32–33, 56–57
crucifixion 47, 77, 90, 95–96
Crusades 38
cuneiform 24, 39
Cyrus the Great 47–48, 51, 62–63

daemon 7, 16–17, 19, 46, 89, 104
David, King 50, 55, 68, 108
de Mello, Anthony 102, 128–129
death 30, 33, 44, 52–53, 67–68, 76, 78–79, 81, 83–84, 86, 89, 92, 95, 102, 112–114, 119–121, 123, 129, 13, 31, 121, 228
demon 17, 43, 46, 63
diaspora 48, 77
Dionysos 94
disobedience 20, 64, 84, 88–89
divine conception 77, 93–94
divinity within 18, 20, 30, 46–47, 66, 69, 72, 76, 82, 93, 96, 98, 101

133

dragon 42, 44–45
Dragonheart (movie) 45
dreams 13, 15–19, 27, 32, 44–45, 104–106, 130, 12, 160
duality 27

Ea 42–43
Eckhart, Meister 80, 98, 100, 109, 127, 130
Eden 24, 33–35, 66, 132
Edman, Irwin 11
Edom 67
Egypt 8, 25, 30, 33, 37, 47, 50–53, 55, 67, 73, 78, 86
Einstein, Albert 99, 105
Eliade, Mircea 27–28, 125, 129
Enki 8, 28–29, 36, 42
Enlil 24, 28
enthousiasmos 18, 20, 76, 96, 109
Enuma Elish 42–44, 46
Eridu Genesis 21, 24, 28, 30, 35, 40
Evagrius 100
Eve 4, 32, 34, 54, 91, 93, 132, 18
Exodus 11, 37, 39, 46, 51–52, 57, 86

fairy tales 19–20, 27, 34, 45, 125, 132
female element 20–21, 35, 66
female figurines 29
Fertile Crescent 24
Francis of Assisi, St 101

Galilee 67–68, 73–74
Garden of Eden 24, 33–35, 66
Genesis 11, 19–21, 24, 26, 28, 30, 32–36, 40, 45, 50, 54, 69, 88, 93, 108
genius 80, 105, 28, 208
genocide 56
Giroud, Francoise 85
Gnostic 80, 92, 98, 127, 131
God 18, 20, 24–29, 31–33, 35–36, 38–39, 42–43, 46–47, 50–52, 58, 60, 63–65, 69, 72–77, 80–83, 86–94, 96–98, 100–103, 106, 110, 122, 126–130, 132, 20, 66
Goddess, see also Great Mother 12, 31, 33, 56, 100
Gospels 7, 9, 55, 64, 66, 72–73, 77–79, 87, 92, 94–96, 127, 130–131
Gray, John 94, 126, 130
Great Flood 36
Great Mother 43–44, 48, 94, 109
Greece, Greek 68
guardian angel 16, 19

Hagar 30, 50
Hammurabi 8, 39, 93
harmony 18, 27–28, 109, 140, 191
Heaven 18, 26–28, 33, 42, 50, 52, 57, 64, 66, 72, 76–77, 79, 94, 100, 112–114, 116, 121–122, 10, 53, 133
Hebrew 18, 20–21, 37–38, 46, 51–55, 57, 62, 75, 86, 94
Hebron 50
Herakles 94
heretic 80, 130
Herod Antipas 67–68, 74
Herod the Great 67, 127, 131
Hitler 38, 138
holiness 18, 26, 47, 98
holy 18, 26, 36, 50, 65, 86–87, 94, 97, 116, 120, 122, 126–128, 131–132
Holy Spirit 65, 94, 97, 116, 122
Hygieia 8, 32

Idumaea 67
inner divinity 46–47, 76, 82, 100–101, 106
inward light 101
Iraq 8, 11, 27, 31, 60
Isaac 46, 50
Ishmael 50
Islam 21, 37, 50, 64–65
Israel 9, 26, 32–34, 48, 50, 53, 55, 57–60, 65, 94, 108, 116

Jacob 26, 46, 50, 56
Jacobsen, Thorkild 36, 44, 46, 125, 130
James 20, 55, 65, 72, 76, 82, 94, 113, 125, 127, 130, 51, 103, 121, 254–256, 264
Jehovah's Witnesses 81
Jerusalem 20, 34, 47–48, 58, 60–62, 65, 67–68, 72, 75–78, 87, 95, 130, 121
Jerusalem sect 77
Jesus 5, 9, 18, 20, 26, 35, 46–47, 51, 54–55, 62, 64–69, 71–83, 86–92, 94–98, 100–101, 106–109, 112–122, 127, 130, 18, 201
Jesus Movement 76–78
Jesus Seminar 9, 79, 130
Jethro 51
John 72–73, 76, 78–79, 87, 90, 94–96, 103, 105, 116, 126, 128–131, 39, 42, 48, 51, 63, 68, 73, 75, 84–88, 90, 119, 167, 181–182, 186, 188, 190, 195, 199, 202, 205, 217, 229–230, 232, 239–240, 250, 254, 262
Josephus 73
Joshua 55–56

INDEX

Josiah 34
Judaeus, Philo 75
Judah 9, 34, 58–60, 65, 67, 94
Judaism 21, 37, 64–65, 68–69, 76–78, 82, 86, 88
Judea 67, 117
Jung, Carl 12, 16, 28, 32, 46, 56, 98, 103, 125, 130

Keturah 51
Ki 24, 28, 30
Kingdom of God 18, 20, 46, 58, 76–77, 81–82, 98
Kingu 42–43
Koester, Helmut 78, 121, 127
Kronos 25

Lao Tzu 94
Last Judgement 64, 76
LeShan, Lawrence 97, 101, 107, 128, 131
Levi 51
love 20, 26, 32, 35, 37, 45, 76, 82, 96, 98, 101, 109, 114, 120–121, 123, 125, 128–129, 131, 7, 28–29, 69, 93, 100–103, 118, 132, 135, 159, 163, 171–172, 174–175, 180, 236
Luke, Gospel of 18, 66, 78, 94
Luther, Martin 74

Mackenzie, Donald 30, 39, 73, 125, 131
Mahy, Margaret 105
male priesthood 92
Mandela, Nelson 68, 83
Marduk 8, 42–48
Mark, Gospel of 18, 75, 77–78
Matthew, Gospel of 18, 78, 94
McCarthyism 38
meditation 5, 96, 102, 123–124
Merton, Thomas 98, 128, 131
Midianites 51
Miller, George 103
miracles 73–74, 93, 130–131
Mohammed 50, 68
Monoimus, Gnostic 80, 98
Moses 20, 24, 33, 37, 39, 46, 51–52, 55, 64, 78
Mother Earth 24, 26, 29–30, 93, 100
Mother Goddess 24, 29–30, 34, 39, 44, 100
Mother Nature 30, 44, 93, 100
Mount Sinai 39, 52
Myers, Briggs 16
mysticism 18, 72, 98, 100, 102, 124, 128, 132
mythical defamation 38

Nag Hammadi 78, 121, 127, 131
Nammu 24, 29–30
Nazareth 67, 74, 94
Near East 12, 21, 24–26, 29, 33, 53, 56
Nebuchadnezzar II 47
New Testament 11, 54, 78–79, 88–89, 95, 98
New Zealand 4, 15, 25, 91, 4, 7, 9, 11, 28, 30–31, 35–36, 38–39, 42–43, 45–47, 49, 51–52, 54, 58, 63–64, 66, 68–71, 74, 80–87, 94–95, 97, 113, 122–125, 128, 138, 141, 143, 147–148, 150, 154, 157, 159–162, 165–167, 169, 171, 174–175, 177, 181–182, 186, 196, 205, 207–210, 213, 216–219, 221, 224, 229–230, 232–233, 236–237, 240, 246–247, 253
Nicene Creed 5, 97, 122
Nietzsche, Friedrich 97
Nile 25, 50, 52
Ninhursag 29–30

obedience 19, 43, 81, 84
Old Testament 11, 26–27, 34–35, 45–46, 48, 52–54, 56–57, 65–66, 75, 86, 97–98
opiate 96
Original Sin 89–91
Ormazd 63–64
Otto, Rudolf 52, 101, 126, 131
Ouranos 25

paganism 45–46
Pagels, Elaine 78, 91, 127, 131
Palestine 9, 57, 75
Paradise 24, 34, 89, 114
Parker, Theodore 88, 127
Parsees 65
Passover 86, 95
Paul 20, 47, 54, 64, 69, 76–79, 81, 84, 86–87, 89, 92–94, 96–97, 129–130, 132, 42, 50, 55, 75–78, 88, 102, 106, 119, 132, 146, 154, 161, 164, 191, 195, 202, 211, 216–217
Persia 8, 25, 62, 65, 68
personal deity 46, 50, 52, 98
Personal myths 15–16, 19
Peter 7, 72, 76–77, 97, 113, 121, 130, 63–64, 78, 119, 154, 216, 224
Pharaoh 30, 51–52
Pharisee 20, 65
Philistines 56–57
Philo Judaeus 75
philosophers 123
Plato 16–19, 44, 66, 76, 98, 100, 109, 125
Pontius Pilate 67, 122

Pope, Alexander 83
pre-god 52
projection 107
Protestantism 90
Proverbs 65–66, 109
psyche 19, 40, 44–45, 98, 103, 106, 109, 140

Quakers 101

regeneration 26–27
Rehoboam 58
Reimarus, Hermann 96
resurrection 47, 64, 76, 94, 96–97, 122
Richards, Keith 105
ritual 26, 44, 86–87
Romans 26, 47, 63, 67–68, 74, 82, 84, 89, 94–97

sacredness 93, 109
sacrifice 20, 51, 73, 78, 86–87, 90, 93, 96, 150, 160, 178, 180, 214, 226
Samaria 58, 67
Samaritans 65, 72, 82
Sarah 30, 50
Sargon 37–38, 51
Saul 57
saviour 43, 64, 76, 84, 90, 96
Schleiermacher, Friedrich 83
Science 40, 74, 97, 103, 108, 125, 130, 38, 52, 61
scientific 103, 105
Sennacherib 58, 60
Sepphoris 67–68, 74, 76
Serpent 32–34, 42, 45, 66
shadow 106–107, 161, 212
Shamash 39
Shishkak 30
Shrek (movie) 45
Siegel, Bernie 17, 104, 125, 131
Simon 68, 113, 121, 130, 182
sin 11–12, 20–21, 45, 84, 86–91, 96, 113, 120
slingers 57
snake, see serpent
Socrates 89
Solomon 30, 34, 47, 57–58
soul 16, 18, 44–45, 64, 66, 76, 80–83, 90, 98, 100, 103, 114–115, 119, 121, 123–125, 130, 66
star 64, 94, 104, 63, 157, 161, 208, 235
Star Wars 104
Stevenson, Robert Louis 105
Sumer 5, 11–12, 21, 23–27, 29, 31–32, 35–40, 46, 48, 50–51, 93, 96, 98, 125, 132

symbol 27–29, 32
Syria 30, 53, 57, 67

Taoism 94
Ten Commandments 52
Terrorism 67–68, 95
Tertullian 91
Thera 52, 57
Thomas, Gospel of 5, 78–79, 82–83, 98, 112, 121, 127
Tiamat 8, 42–44
Tigris and Euphrates Rivers 24–25, 29
Tree of Life 8, 17, 33–34, 66, 88

unconscious 16–20, 36, 44, 54, 100, 103–106, 108–109
Underhill, Evelyn 101–102, 124, 128, 132
unity 12, 26–27, 43, 98, 101, 124, 139
Ur 11, 21, 37

virgin birth 94
visions 104–105
vocation 17
von Franz, Marie-Louise 20, 125, 132
vote to women 91

war 20, 43–44, 56, 60, 68, 97, 101, 107, 113, 128, 131, 16, 67, 79, 81, 126, 138, 140
Warka 8, 27, 31
wholeness 18, 24, 28, 40, 44, 65, 98, 101, 109, 125
Wisdom 15–17, 19, 28, 32–34, 44–45, 48, 58, 65–66, 74, 100, 104, 109
women 12, 21, 30, 39–40, 53–56, 58, 64, 91–93, 101, 116, 121, 7, 38, 126, 165, 172, 224, 257
World Mountain 24–25, 39

Yahweh 19–20, 28, 32, 35–36, 43, 46, 50–53, 55–56, 58, 60, 62, 76, 98
yin and yang 8, 28, 44, 101, 109

zealots 68
Zeus 94
ziggurat 8, 26–27, 29
Zion, see Jerusalem
Zipporah 51
Zoroaster 51, 63–64, 94
Zoroastrians 65, 96, 129